THE BALLOON GIRL

THE FIRST AND FATAL FLIGHT OF
MADEMOISELLE ALBERTINA

To Gloria
Best Wishes
Rosemary Chaloner
13th November 2020

ROSEMARY CHALONER

The right of Rosemary Chaloner to be identified as the
Author of the Work has been asserted by her in accordance
with the Copyright, Designs
and Patents Act 1988.

Copyright © Rosemary Chaloner 2019

Cover by Shaun Russell

ISBN: 978-0-9954821-1-1

Published by
Jelly Bean Books
Mackintosh House
136 Newport Road, Cardiff, CF24 1DJ
www.candyjarbooks.co.uk

Printed and bound in the UK by
4Edge Ltd, Essex, SS5 4AD

All rights reserved.
No part of this publication may be reproduced, stored in a
retrieval system, or transmitted at any time or by any means,
electronic, mechanical, photocopying, recording or otherwise
without the prior permission of the copyright holder. This
book is sold subject to the condition that it shall not by way
of trade or otherwise be circulated without the publisher's
prior consent in any form of binding or cover
other than that in which it is published.

For L'um who loved books.

"Life is short, the art long, opportunities fleeting, experiment treacherous and judgement difficult"
                                              Hippocrates

— FAMILY TREES —

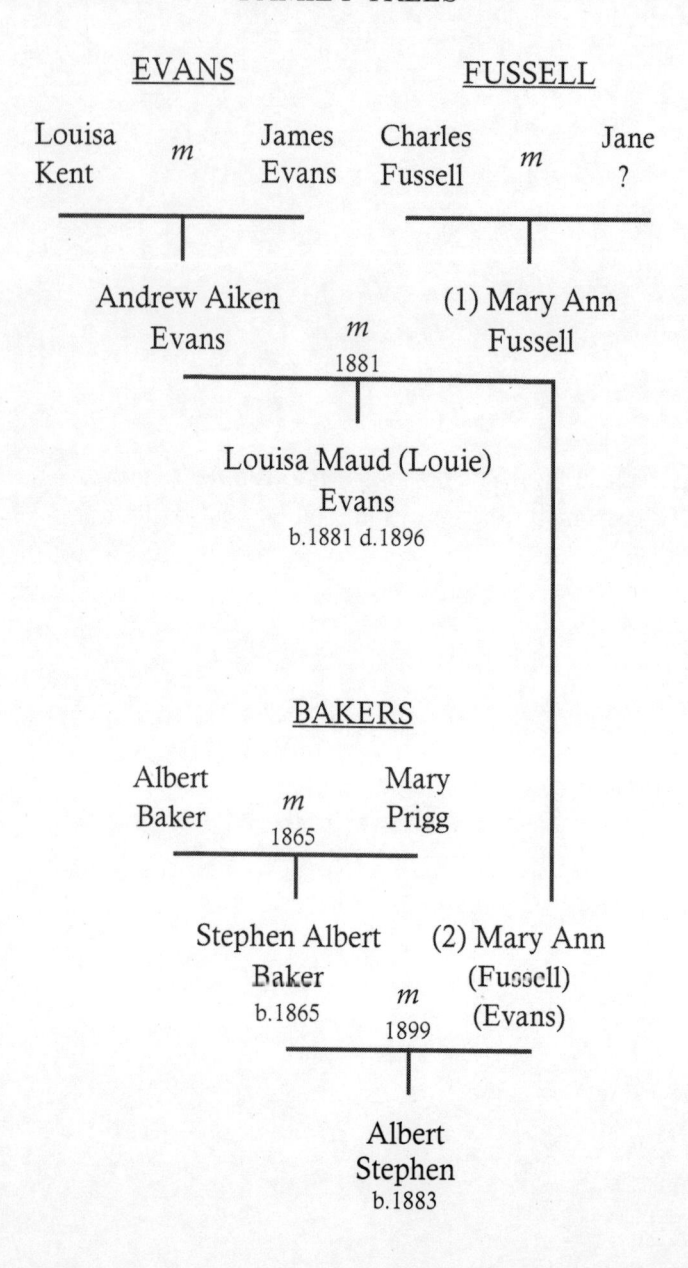

EVANS / FUSSELL

Louisa Kent *m* James Evans

Charles Fussell *m* Jane ?

Andrew Aiken Evans *m* 1881 (1) Mary Ann Fussell

Louisa Maud (Louie) Evans
b.1881 d.1896

BAKERS

Albert Baker *m* 1865 Mary Prigg

Stephen Albert Baker
b.1865
m 1899
(2) Mary Ann (Fussell) (Evans)

Albert Stephen
b.1883

HANCOCKS

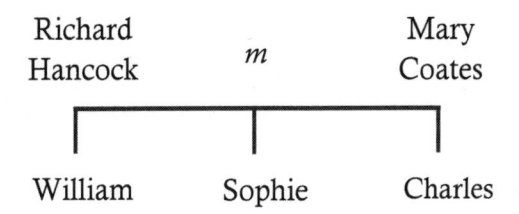

Richard Hancock —m— Mary Coates

- William
- Sophie
- Charles

CRINKS

William Henry Crinks —m 1880— Mary (Prigg) (Baker)

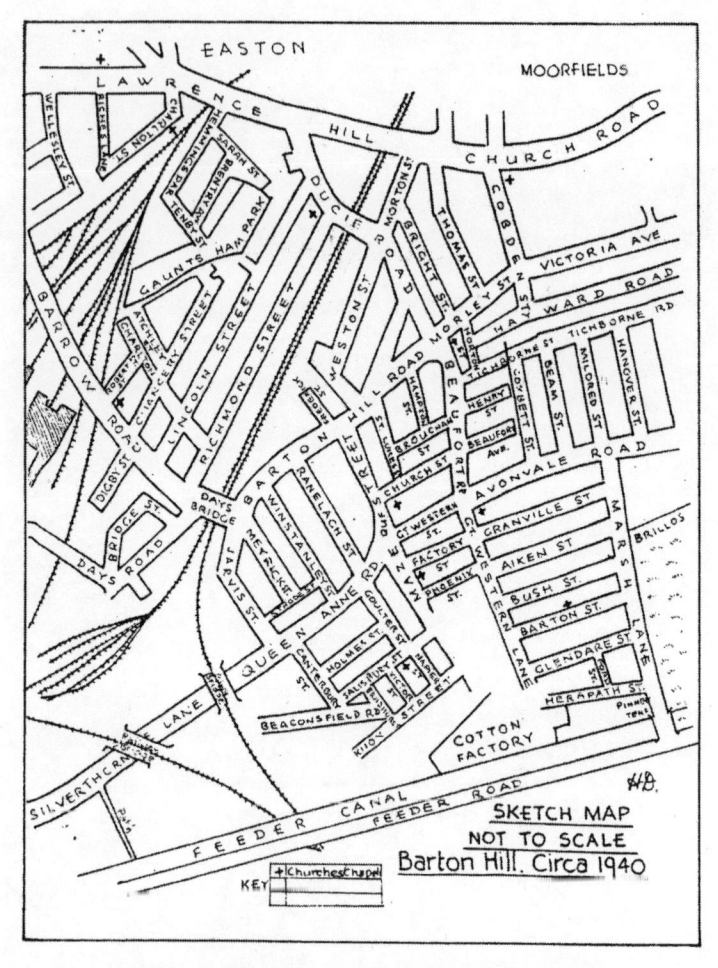

Map showing Barton Hill Road and Queen Anne Road, Bristol

— PROLOGUE —

When Mary Waggett decided to stroll along the banks of the Severn Estuary to search the shoreline for driftwood, she could not have imagined that the events of her early evening walk would cause an outpouring of national sadness; how it would engulf the nation, and the effect it would have on the little Welsh village community of Nash.

As the 7 o'clock sun slid towards the horizon, Mary waved goodbye to her mother and younger siblings, gathered up the reed basket and set out from the family cottage, half a mile to the west of the village. The rays of the late sun lit the quiet country lanes and local schoolhouse. The spire of the medieval village church caught the last of the evening warmth, casting a grey-black shadow over ancient mossy tombstones. The high trees surrounding the village inn towered above her, rivalling the church spire.

Mary turned away from home and headed towards the coast. She followed paths cut deep into soil by familiarity and crossed over farm fields where hay cutters were working late into the evening; the local farmers anxious to have their hay cut and crops stored after a period of indifferent weather. On that Friday evening, the 24th July 1896, the weather had improved after a dull and unsettled start to the day. The late afternoon light faded into evening as the young girl walked towards the salt marshes spread along the seashore.

The land Mary crossed to reach the shore had been reclaimed from the encroaching seas and fresh water streams over many centuries. It had been an avenue into Wales for Roman and Norman invaders as well as a trade route and an area of settlement whose people had left behind a legacy of drainage channels and earthworks. Their artefacts had been discovered after many centuries buried deep in the mudflats and salt marshes so familiar to the area. Two thousand years since legionnaires had toiled to erect a linear earthwork along the edge of the shore; an early defence against the sea, built and rebuilt over the years.

By 1896 a strong defence of boulders and breakwater continued to protect the precious land. During the 13th and 14th centuries, lower lying inland areas had been drained and then enclosed. The fertile land an area of mature trees and cut hedges. Reens, banks, surface drainage and footbridges allowed access to scattered farms and cottages: Redbarn Farm, Cold Harbour, Henton, Saltmarsh, Burnthouse and Cross farms. The fields, small and irregular, were peculiar to the area and bound by sinuous lanes, created dispersed settlements in the agricultural landscape.

To reach the shore Mary passed through these ancient pastures, crossed the reens and water-filled ditches and followed long-established narrow footpaths. Julian's Reen wound its way through meadowland from the Usk River to Burnthouse Farm lying to the north of Nash village. Skinners' Reen meandered south towards the Severn Estuary. Unpredictable narrow waterways scooped deep into the earth. In summer, trickles of water bubbled through sluggish mud banks, the wild flowers and warmth of a summer evening seducing memory. In winter the winds whipped along these channels, barren of colour. Waves of water spilled out over pastures and reed beds.

Storms rushed up the Bristol Channel from the Irish Sea and raced across the open flat pastures buffeting and flattening the remains of reed and marsh plant. Winds swept over ditches and reens; water slapped and smacked against soft mud banks, the narrow footbridges awash with water and silt. A blast of ice-wind could pierce without fear or favour, any carelessly buttoned topcoat or cloak tossing away loose-bound mufflers. Fingers stiff with cold clutched at bonnet or cap and water-filled eyes scrunched tightly in token resistance against winter's onslaught.

Mary's route up the slope of the grassy bank, led towards the sea. She knew the tides would be on the ebb and hoped pieces of timber, suitable to burn on the cottage fires and small enough to fit into her basket, would be within reach.

Wild fowl and wading birds, a common sight on the many waterways, were feeding and nesting in the dense vegetation of marsh plants and head-high reed beds. In wintertime the mudflats became a vast feeding ground for large flocks of wild ducks and geese.

Two lighthouses stood either side of the entrance to the Usk River, each one a reassuring beacon of light warning all shipping of the impending navigational hazards that lay ahead at the Mouth of the Usk, before it wound ultimately to the busy docks at Newport. The uppermost glass of the beacon of the East Usk Lighthouse became visible to Mary as she climbed the grassy slope towards the sea wall, where the Bristol Channel met the mouths of the Severn Estuary and the Usk River, a capricious and at times unpredictable shipping channel. At the top of the bank, the lighthouse stood looking out over the Severn Estuary; a grey expanse of uncompromising sea stretching across to English shores.

Once the bank had been negotiated and the summit reached, a pathway heading either right or left followed the lines of the sea defences. Mary turned left and headed away from the lighthouse walking towards "Iron Railings Bay".

As she had expected the tide was on the ebb, exposing the mudflats, the fine sands of the salt-flats and sea-drenched grey-green vegetation. Seawater lapped against huge boulders that supported the wall. Timber and flotsam lay over the mud and in the marsh plants, small planks and branches were wedged between the boulders. Detritus littered the shoreline from the many ships that sailed up the channel to Clevedon and eventually to the ancient trading port of Bristol.

Mary walked on towards Goldcliff Bay, a mile or so in the distance, still searching for timber along the water's edge. The evening sun cast strange shadows on the sea as it sank below the horizon, distorting the object moving in and out with the tide. Mary paused, raising inquisitive eyes towards the water. A halo of light from the dipping sun's rays bruised the cluster of waves that gathered beneath the unholy sight. Mary watched in disbelief as the blue-clad body floated nearer to the shore, its boot-shod feet resting briefly on the fine sand. Rooted by fear and shocked by the awful sight of the bobbing corpse she peeped through fingers stiff with fright as the reed basket tumbled and bumped over the damp boulders.

The young girl thought it was a sailor. The clothing covering the upper part of the body resembled a naval uniform and a cork life belt appeared to be tied across each shoulder and secured tightly around the body. Frightened by what she had found, staring in disbelief and uncertain as to what she should do next, she hesitated, shivered, then turned her back on the sea and ran.

Will Little had paused his rhythmic cutting of hay, he rested the scythe against his body and wiped sweat from his moist hands. He glanced towards the distant sea wall as a small girl, who seemed in some distress, ran towards him. He recognised her as one of the young daughters of ferryman, William Waggett. The girl, pale and trembling, fair hair escaping from beneath her summer bonnet caught her breath before explaining what she had seen: a body floating in the sea near the East Usk lighthouse.

Something needed to be done. He resolved to retrace the route Mary had taken an hour previously to assess the situation for himself.

Whilst he did not doubt the young girl's agitation was genuine, he wanted to determine for himself that her story of finding a body was not just that of a child's fanciful imagination. He reasoned that the evening sun could cast strange shapes at dusk and floating timber easily mistaken for something more sinister.

Despite a mounting reluctance, Mary agreed to return with him. She walked steadily ahead of the hay cutter whilst searching the water's edge. After some time had passed and some distance covered, she paused, then pointed towards the rocky outcrop where little pools of foamy water had been left behind by the tide as it receded. The body now lay sprawled on the large stones at the bottom of the earth banking.

Scrambling over the sea wall and down the bank in the gathering gloom, he reached the lifeless figure. He was careful not to disturb anything before calling to Mary to run home just as quickly as she could and inform her parents of the discovery.

A local newspaper would later report, "At about 10 o'clock on the evening of 24th young Mary Waggett saw a body on the mud at the side of the entrance to the Usk River.

She then gave information to her parents, who communicated with P.C. Boucher, the local police constable." A further report published on the same day in the same newspaper informed, "It was first seen floating in the water by the little girl Mary Waggett, she then ran home to tell her mother who despatched a messenger for the police." On Monday 27th another report informed its readers, "As early as 8 o'clock on Friday evening a little girl named Mary Waggett saw a body floating in the water. She spoke about it to her mother who told her to go up to the public house at Nash [The Waterloo Inn] and make it known to the men there and they would tell the police."

Differences occurred in essentials from one news report to another. *The South Wales Echo* claimed, "The body was found lying in a slanting position upon its back, the arms thrown out, the head being towards the shore and feet towards the water." Another reported, "The head being towards the water and feet towards the shore." One fact was certain, however, this young girl had found the body not of a sailor but of an aeronaut: a casualty of public expectation, who had launched from the grounds of the prestigious Fine Arts Exhibition taking place eight miles away in Cardiff. Missing since the evening of Tuesday 21st July, this discovery by Mary Waggett had solved, in part, the mystery of a young girl's disappearance three days earlier. A disappearance that had consumed public interest with rumour and conjecture flamed by extensive press reports and speculation.

Mademoiselle Albertina had been found.

— CHAPTER ONE —

There is no recorded evidence to suggest that the circumstances of Louisa Maud Evan's birth was in any way unusual or dramatic. The same cannot be said of her death.

On the 6th December 1881, Mary Ann Evans was delivered of a baby girl, Louisa Maud, the firstborn to Mary Ann and her husband Andrew. Louisa's birth was registered at Barton Regis District, in Bristol during January 1882. She was baptised eight months later on 27th August, at the church of St. Lukes in Queen Anne Road.

The young couple married in January 1881, in the same Barton Regis District; one of several Poor Law Unions established in 1834, and responsible for all things administrative: births, marriages and deaths. This district comprised of fifteen parishes one of which, St. Philip and Jacob Out, where Mary Ann, born in 1863, had lived with her parents Charles and Jane Fussell until her marriage to Andrew Evans.

Andrew was born in Birkenhead, Cheshire on 24th September 1860. His mother Louisa Kent had married

James Evans, a Merchant Navy seaman, a year or two previously. However, by 1871 eleven-year-old Andrew was living with his mother's brother, Alfred Kent and his wife Elizabeth, at 9 Victoria Terrace, Bristol, in the same district as Mary Ann. The reason for this has not been established.

There are no written records to indicate how Mary Ann and Andrew met. They could have become friendly as children or through the close proximity of their houses and the schools they would have attended; and of course the neighbourliness of families. They were married when Mary Ann was just eighteen and Andrew twenty-one. Four years earlier, Andrew had joined Her Majesty's Royal Navy as a naval cadet, on 24th September 1876, his 16th birthday. Following in the footsteps of his father.

He began cadet training aboard HMS *Implacable*, based at Devonport Docks, in Plymouth.
The vessel was an ancient survivor of the 1805 Battle of Trafalgar and later designated a training ship for young boys. Andrew was described on his naval records as 5'6" in height, with light brown hair, grey eyes, a fair complexion and with a scar on his right cheek.

The Royal Naval sailed the seven seas protecting Britain's vast Empire and diverse interests. Andrew, a part of this great armada, would return to his family for brief respite until summoned to another ship and another tour of duty; at the end of each tour the fleet were welcomed back to their home ports of Portsmouth or Plymouth. Although Andrew's homeport of Bristol was not a designated naval base, its busy docks welcomed trading ships from across the Empire. Steam and sails billowed proudly as they glided up the Bristol Channel, past the impressive Bute Docks at Cardiff and the glowing smoke-red chimneys of Dowlais Steel works, towards the historic West Country port.

Bristol has a rich heritage and its maritime history is both controversial and heroic.

The slave trade, historically recorded as beginning at the end of the 14th century, became prolific during the 1640s.

It was at its most extreme universally in the 18th century with Bristol playing a central role. Sailing ships plied back and forth between Bristol, the colonies and Africa. Ships' holds on their outward journeys were filled with woollen materials, brass and iron goods manufactured in Bristol's factories and workshops; human cargo was the ballast of choice on return sailings. Wealthy West Country merchants saw the opportunity to invest in this unseemly trade. Their financial gains expanded the wealth and boundaries of the city, which brought extraordinary prosperity, fuelling in part the Industrial Revolution. The trade in slavery was also perpetrated in Wales by men and women greedy for the increased wealth it would bring them. An opportunity to make huge profits from slavery, through ownership of plantations in foreign climes, shipping and transportation of the thousands of sad souls ripped from their native lands, was a temptation too great to ignore.

By the late 18th and early 19th centuries William Wilberforce and the anti-slavery lobbyists raised the conscience of the country. Encouraged by the fervour of Wilberforces' campaign, at the commencement of the 19th century this unseemly trade ceased. The city's image underwent a radical change and by the middle of the 1800s boasted a bustling port, the second largest after London.

Fame followed infamy, masterminded by one of its adopted sons. Suffering serious injury whilst working on the construction of the Thames Tunnel in London, the industrious and extraordinary Victorian Engineer Isambard Kingdom Brunel sought to recuperate from his injuries in Bristol. The city, the West Country and South Wales became beneficiaries of his brilliance. Isambard's designs, some of which were considered controversial at times, became lynch pins of the Industrial Revolution, a bloodless revolution that galloped unchecked across the length and breadth of Britain. Ships and bridges were built, railway tracks criss-crossed countryside, steam locomotives sped through rural idylls, the rush of town and city captured in broad brushstrokes of smoke and coal-fuelled engines. Brunel's genius would secure him international fame and lasting celebrity.

Bristol, as many seaports, was a place of social interaction, meetings and marriages. Sadly, Mary Ann and Andrew Aiken would not have the fairytale ending this young couple envisaged on their wedding day.

Between 1882 and 1883 records suggest Mary Ann became involved with a friend of the family, a young man she had known for several years, the affair resulting in a pregnancy. These Victorian participants, anxious to conceal their actions, found honesty an uncomfortable bedfellow.

Faced with the tragedy that was to occur in the summer of 1896, facts were fudged, the truth manipulated.

She sought the help of her near neighbours William and Mary Crinks and together the two families rewrote the truth. Louisa's father Andrew would be vilified as having deserted his wife and baby. Yet contemporary naval records, as previously referred to, showed that he was serving as an able-bodied seaman, aboard HMS *Dragon*. His character was given as "Very Good": he had not disappeared. He could have been traced.

Had he deserted his young family, or left them without financial support, could contact have been made either through the Admiralty or directly to the ship on which he was serving? Were there problems within the marriage prior to November 1882? Had he refused to support his wife and child due to Mary's affair? Many questions all without definitive answers.

Whatever the truth, his baby daughter Louisa Maud, the innocent in this "penny dreadful" mess, would be shuffled from person to person and place to place.

Before any of these events, Mary Ann and Andrew Evans, then recently married, were living in their first marital home in Bristol: a few rented rooms in a terraced house at 31 Barton Hill Road. An area where once fertile farmland and winding hills sloped up to grassy fields and shallow streams once flowed, all now eaten up by urbanisation.

The Evans' initially enjoyed the privacy to explore their married life together and were overjoyed at the prospect of their baby, due in December. Although by mid-April, four months after the marriage, Andrew's naval career had intervened. He was at sea once again, serving aboard HMS *Royal Adelaide*. The April census of 1881 indicates that Mary Ann had returned to live with her parents, Charles and Jane Fussell, and her six younger siblings, at 18 Sharlands Court. (Unfortunately no reference to the location of Sharlands Court now exists.)

She was then three months pregnant. Andrew remained at sea until the beginning of May, when there was an opportunity for the young couple to spend a few days together, before he was recalled on 10th May to attend a training program.

Whilst her parents were a support to their eighteen-year-old daughter, it conjures up an image of cramped conditions, with four brothers and two sisters, the eldest aged twenty and the youngest child only a few months old.

Andrew's naval records show he may have taken shore leave in early December as the birth of their baby approached. Louisa Maud, was born on 6th December.

Within a few days of Louisa Maud's birth, Andrew

was again at sea. With the approach of Christmas this young mother faced the prospects of spending the festive season alone. The friendliness shown by her neighbours William and Mary Crinks and Mary's son Stephen proved to be most welcome.

Stephen, then seventeen and close in age to Mary Ann and Andrew, welcomed the association and took advantage of opportunities to seek out the young couple's company. Intimate friendships would develop, lasting for many years.

Sixteen months after the birth of little Lousia, Andrew was on the other side of the world, serving aboard HMS *Dragon*, when it was reported he had deserted his family, leaving them penniless and in a desperate state.

Women in this situation in Victorian Britain would have few choices: either the workhouse, destitution or prostitution. Although contemporary records revealed this ultimately would not be the outcome, Mary Ann decided upon an equally drastic solution. During the spring of 1883 she determined to give her baby away. Louisa Maud would have to be adopted.

Let us pursue other options. If the young woman was in dire financial straits, perhaps her previous employers, Baker's Portable Theatre company based in Kingswood near Bristol, could be approached. However, the troupe spent several months of each year travelling and performing throughout the West Country. How would she look after her baby daughter? Although her parents and older siblings lived nearby, there is no evidence to suggest that she appealed to them for assistance, or that her family offered to help their daughter and granddaughter.

And so she approached William and Mary Crinks and begged them to take her baby. The Crinks were surprisingly anxious to offer Mary Ann and Louisa their support. As well as being neighbours, the two women were acquainted through their acting profession, both having appeared with the same theatre company.

But given what is known, the arrangement to adopt Louisa Maud in 1883 was more than a generous act of neighbourly largesse by the Crinks family. It was prompted by a complication of relationships, illegitimacy and marriages. Loyalty bound these people to one another even more strongly than the need to tell the truth or to deny false accusations.

— CHAPTER TWO —

Louisa's unofficial adoption by the Crinks caused her no dislocation from familiarity. She continued to live in the same area of Bristol with her adoptive parents, just two doors away from where she had lived with her parents. Despite her decision to change Louisa's life so drastically,

Mary Ann remained in contact with her baby daughter.

However it seemed initially that the child had no further contact with her father. The only recorded comments relating to Andrew and his relationship with his wife were made by William Crinks. These unsubstantiated accusations of Andrew having deserted his family, whether true or false, gained validation with William's reported comments. Justification for his bias against Andrew Evans, however, has not been established and none of the records unearthed during research indicate whether Andrew ever challenged these accusations.

What were William Crinks' motives when he denounced Louisa's father as deserting his family? A man he may have known only as a near neighbour for a few months.

Mary Ann would have given the Crinks legitimate

grounds for her behaviour and reasons enough for them to adopt her daughter. Although the break-up of the marriage was recorded controversially as desertion by her husband,perhaps the reason was rooted not in Andrew's behaviour but in Mary Ann's infidelity.

The families involved could not have envisaged that over one hundred years later, their story would be subject to extensive research, research that would reveal intimate details of their lives. The truth had been manipulated in order to uphold family reputations. Exposure of such scandalous behaviour could have breached the code of Victorian morality, and so Andrew's character had to be sacrificed and loyalty to blood relations upheld at all costs.

Louisa too was embroiled in these deceptions: falsifying her name and parentage. When challenged several years later about her relatives, Louisa said she had not seen her mother for many years and believed her to be dead, which was untrue, referring to her "only living relative" as a grandmother living in Bilston. Initially believed to be a corruption of Bristol, further research however revealed Andrew's mother, Louisa Evans, did live at Bilston in Staffordshire. Contact with her father and paternal grandmother may have survived the adoption after all. Louisa would no doubt have been instructed that any thoughtless admission by her about birth parents or her real name could have brought the whole sham crashing down on them all.

William and Mary's willingness to adopt (unofficially) the little daughter of their young actress friend, was undoubtedly an act of exceeding neighbourliness. These good people were in their mid-thirties at the time of the adoption. So was taking a toddler into their household a hindrance? Restricting their itinerant working lives? Such commitment and devotion to the child of a near neighbour needed an explanation.

A bewildering complexity of marriages and relationships renders some understandable confusion. So many similarities: Mary Evans and Mary Crinks both actresses who worked with Bakers Portable Theatre. Both young women who chose to marry when they were in their teens.

Mary Crinks (nee Prigg) was married initially to Albert Baker in Swansea sometime between January and March 1865; she was seventeen years of age, he was twenty-two. Later that same year she gave birth to their son Stephen Albert, whilst the couple were living at Malpas near Newport in South Wales. The 1871 census records the family as then residing at The Pontypool Arms, Pontypool. Seven years later the death of Albert in December 1878 rendered Mary Baker a widow.

In 1880, two years later, official records in Bristol confirmed a marriage, between Mary Baker and William Henry Crinks. By the following year the couple and Mary's son Stephen, (from her first marriage to Albert Baker) had settled in at 35 Barton Hill Road, on the outskirts of Bristol, an area of rapid, thrusting industrial development creating an unimpressive tangle of factories and railway lines, bridges and terraced housing, and just a few doors away from Mary Ann and Andrew Evans.

One year later, a dramatic change in circumstances also affected Mary Ann and one-year-old Louisa Maud. In December 1882, Mary Ann had left the rented rooms at 31 Barton Hill Road that she and Andrew had shared since their wedding. From early November Andrew's naval duties had demanded he sign on again with another ship. He had been recently promoted to Able-bodied Seaman aboard HMS *Dragon* and this extensive tour of duty would not be completed until 22nd August 1884. Were his long absences at sea cause enough for the breakdown of their marriage?

Several months after Andrew had rejoined his ship, Mary Ann gave birth to a baby boy. He was named Albert.

A few months prior to the birth of Albert, Mary Evans had approached the Crinks to ask if they would consider "adopting" Louisa Maud. Would Andrew have been advised of these two dramatic events? Was baby Albert Andrew's son? Or had the couple already agreed to separate before he sailed with HMS *Dragon* the previous November? And did he agree to his little daughter, Louisa, being adopted by a thirty-five-year-old near neighbour? It has not been possible to find information confirming whether he was ever told. We do know that by the time of the 1891 Census, Andrew had retired from the navy (in 1888) after twelve years of service and was no longer living at Barton Hill. The Crinks family too had moved from Barton Hill Road. William, Mary and Louisa Maud Evans, now ten years old and by then known as Louie Crinks, were residing at 93 Queen Anne Road. A short walk from the church of St. Lukes where she had been christened and the home at

Barton Hill Road she had shared with her parents nine years before. It was these complex family relationships that were partially responsible for the tragedy that would soon befall them.

The Crinks remained in the Barton Hill district, initially with Mary's son Stephen.

By the middle of 1883, the dynamics of the household had changed. Stephen, then eighteen years of age no longer lived with his mother and stepfather. He had his own family to support, and his contribution towards the Crinks' family finances ceased. Could the demands of looking after Louie eventually become a drain on their limited resources?

This close, extraordinary friendship between William, Mary and Stephen, and Mary Ann and Louie, had developed significantly during 1881 and 1882 when the two families shared the same neighbourhood, the same hardships and the same daily effort to survive.

As the bells of St. Luke's church rang out, ushering in the New Year, the families living in row upon row of back-to-back terraces in Barton Hill may have greeted 1883 with a renewed sense of optimism; the happy expectations that each New Year brings. The Evans and Crinks, eager to embrace the future, could not have foreseen how the future would destroy their world. The Crinks family, a complexity of an adopted child; a second marriage; two children, Stephen and Louie, unrelated, living in cramped lodgings and supported by a stepfather who had no blood ties to either child. Yet, despite all the problems that could have arisen, William and Mary did their best for their family; as much as their circumstances and financial considerations permitted. These were strong, caring people, struggling against unimaginable odds, during the latter part of the 19th century.

Those in penury during Victorian England suffered extreme hardship, as Mary Evans, Louie's mother, could have discovered had she had no apparent means of supporting a small child.

In response to a Poor Law Commission established in 1832, set up to investigate the distribution of Poor Relief, a national programme was approved and instigated two years later in 1834. This programme realised a rigorously implemented regime centred round the introduction of a new model: the Workhouse. The emphasis placed on curtailing financial dependency of the poor and destitute from receipt of Parish relief. This ruling would depend primarily on the speedy conversion of hospitals and premises deemed suitable as workhouses. A further programme was approved with indecent haste to build workhouses within the newly established Parish "Union" and this resulted in the amalgamation of ancient parish boundaries. No challenges were forthcoming and if anyone had the temerity to object these complaints were swept aside by a tidal wave of indifference.

This new initiative would replace the financial regulations, or Poor Relief System, in England and Wales which had existed under a variety of titles since Medieval and Tudor times: the original Poor Law was passed in the reign of Elizabeth I to deal with the "impotent poor". It was parish-based and administered locally, the implementation of which, was to say the least, regarded as haphazard. The administrative system would change dramatically when the Poor Law Union Amendment Act became law in 1834 throughout the two countries.

The aim of the 1834 Act was to cease all financial assistance for those unfortunates unable to support themselves in England and Wales. The New Administration's intention was to enforce a rigorous regime implemented centrally and imposed on every impoverished soul a third of which, records show, were over sixty-five years of age.

The daunting workhouse system would provide accommodation and employment, instead of apportioning individual financial assistance to those in need, as had been the case prior to 1834. This new Act would prohibit the provision of relief to anyone who refused to enter these institutions. No able-bodied person would receive money or assistance from the Poor Law Authorities except within the new system of the Workhouse.

These stringent conditions were intended to force the destitute amongst the population to become self-sufficient and "stand on their own two feet". Workhouse conditions were made "less desirable" to those seeking financial support and anyone begging for assistance would be considered as "lacking the moral determination to survive".

During the next few years, at least seven hundred

workhouses were established throughout England and Wales, where the worst fears of potential inmates would be only too well realised.

On arrival at a designated workhouse, families were segregated, husbands from wives, children from parents with no allowance made for the age of the child. The bonds that united, strengthened and supported a family were crushed immediately by the sudden separation, a psychological strategy to strip inmates of their dignity. There were no exceptions. It was a brutal regime.

Vagrant Wards were set up as a separate system in the 1840s to remove the penniless and the beggars from the streets. Inmates who lacked working skills would be set to break stones or crush bone for fertiliser. A dreadful and hated task was the unpicking of Oakum: coils of old sea-soaked, tar-matted rope that had to be untwisted and separated into individual strands, until each resisting strand was pulled and picked apart by hands left blistered and bleeding. To separate the strands a large nail called a spike could be used. As a result of which, workhouses became known colloquially as the "Spike". Some with a more ironic turn of phrase referred to it as the "Bastille".

All incumbents were expected to work in order to pay for their food and bed, usually labouring ten hours a day. Children, imprisoned sometimes for a minor misdemeanour, were made to perform these same tasks too. No leniency was shown for age, whether very young or very old. Sparse meals consisted of gruel and bread, occasionally supplemented with small portions of meat. If the incumbents refused to accede to these rules and regulations the authorities could refuse admittance, forcing destitution on masses of the population.

This Act completely dismantled the centuries-old distribution of ad-hoc financial assistance administered by the parishes to the needy. Replaced with a highly centralised system, this large-scale development of workhouses saw the rise of unimaginable hardship leading to dire consequences. Thousands suffered within the newly created and universally hated system. Destitution was visited upon thousands of other poverty struck souls who were refused admission even to these sad solutions to human misery. Criticism was voiced by ministers of the various churches and politicians of both the Whig and Tory parties.

A Victorian author was so incensed by his perceived injustice against the poor and needy he wrote a novel that shocked society. Railing against the Poor Law Amendment Act, the dominance of the Workhouse system, and its effect on families and on children in particular. The novel was *Oliver Twist*; the author Charles Dickens.

The plight of people unable to be financially self-sufficient was pitiful. However, towards the end of the 19th century the role of the workhouse shifted significantly as the elderly, sick and infirm sought refuge within these institutions. After fifty years the emphasis had moved away from shaming, curtailing financial assistance and denying inmates dignity. In 1929 new legislation was passed abolishing Workhouses and control of the system became the responsibility of local authorities. Many of the old workhouses throughout England and Wales were transformed into much needed local hospitals. This sad episode in the two countries' history was retained in the buildings' forbidding facades.

William and Mary's situation, whilst in need of a resolution, was not so dire as to have necessitated placing Louie in a workhouse. By then her mother Mary Ann had returned to Barton Hill and was living with her new family a stone's throw away from her daughter and the Crinks. There is nothing to suggest she ever offered to reclaim her young daughter. Neither did she seem to offer the Crinks any practical or financial assistance.

Once Louie's education was completed it would be expeditious to find paid employment. And with this in mind William Crinks began to make plans. The young girl could find work in one of the cotton or cloth factories close by. Or perhaps their friend and sometime employer William Hancock would become the solution to their situation and to Louie's future.

— CHAPTER THREE —

William and Mary Crinks were always delighted to receive an invitation from their old friend William Hancock, popular West Country showman and entrepreneur. A request to socialise with the head of the Hancock Dynasty was an offer they would not refuse.

William, an itinerant fairground gilder and painter, and Mary, a professional actress, usually visited the Hancock brothers, William and Charles and their sister Sophie when in need of paid employment. Contemporary records suggest on this occasion, however, they had something more pressing and personal on their minds. They wanted to discuss the future of their adopted daughter, a delicate matter no doubt broached with a degree of hesitation and diplomacy. They hoped William Hancock would perhaps consider employing her as a companion to his wife Sophie.

These two families' lifestyles were polarised by their circumstances: one enjoyed success, the trappings of celebrity and financial security whilst the other was itinerant and dependent on casual employment. How the Crinks must have admired and perhaps envied the

Hancocks. Should their proposal for the girl be agreed upon, this would be an opportunity for her to travel within a secure family environment; an opportunity for Louie to live and work with the famous West Country showman, and a chance for her to enjoy a life with "prospects" far removed from her daily grind working in a cotton cloth factory in Bristol.

Unskilled girls had little choice of employment, with most seeking work in domestic service or factories; repetitive, soulless and exhausting labour. And although Louie was literate, she was unskilled. She had attended school in Bristol, at the fine three-story red brick edifice dominating the lower end of Queen Anne Road in Barton Hill, until her formal education ceased officially in July of 1895.

Once her education had finished, she did in fact find employment at Todd's Clothing Factory where she laboured six days of the week as one of several young Cloth Girls.

Although every Sunday was a welcome day of rest, families would be expected to attend services at their local church at least once during the day, with their children attending the local Sunday school. This was a universal routine, as natural in its acceptance by the population as the drawing in and exhaling of each breath.

Louie performed the same daily routine. Every morning at daybreak, throughout the warm summer months, autumn's gold-edged days and winter's fractious cold she walked the familiar, unsurprising narrow terraced streets, beneath grime-clogged railway arches, past smoking factory chimneys, towards her employment. The only reward at the end of her working week: meagre wages supplementing the Crinks' income.

Life, however, was soon to change dramatically for both Louie and the Crinks. They had raised her as their own for many years, now they were offering her as a domestic helper to the Hancocks.

The travelling fair and menagerie owned by the two Hancock brothers and their larger-than-life sister Sophie was the epitome of a successful Victorian family business. They had worked diligently over the years to reap the rich rewards of fame and success, their popularity throughout the West Country was now second to none. These Victorian entrepreneurs could attract record crowds to the fun of the fair and their fetes, from the tin mining towns of Cornwall to the rural pastures of Gloucester. Wherever publicity posters appeared, this extraordinary family's arrival guaranteed thousands of visitors. Children who were excited by the sight of brightly coloured posters would plead for pennies to spend on the magical whirling fairground rides or the hoopla stalls. William, ever the astute businessman, enjoyed the role of jolly extrovert, captain of the good ship "Hancock" who encouraged the crowds, extolling the pleasures of the fair. Megaphone in hand, his voice, ringing out over the fairground, dominated the ornate, wooden-carved platform of the popular marvel of the day: the Bioscope.

Charles, less outgoing than his flamboyant brother, suffered with indifferent health during his adult years, and was the quieter businessman who supported William in all financial matters, whilst their sister Sophie – of whom it was often said had a face that was certainly "not her fortune" – kept a benevolent eye on the extended family, her bearing dominating the fairgrounds with energy and humour.

By contrast William and Mary Crinks constantly sought paid employment with the circuses and fairs that arrived in their hometown of Bristol, at times travelling throughout the West Country and South Wales. Most towns boasted a free library where copies of local newspapers were available and could be scoured for work, but word of mouth amongst the travelling community provided options for them too. Mary Crinks could boast of relatives who achieved professional renown as lion tamers, trapeze artists and wire walkers, and was perhaps determined to maintain the tradition of these famous ancestors.

Why did the Crinks request Louie become part of the Hancock entourage at that precise time? Was their decision influenced by an unexpected opportunity offered to them during the previous year? Or had they become tired of the constant travelling to find work?

They had brought the little girl up for the past thirteen years. Should the Hancocks take the girl as a domestic servant, it would relieve them of further responsibility, changing again the direction of this young woman's life,

Her future determined once more by those closest to her. And so Louie was handed over to another family, yet again. A Victorian game of "pass the inconvenient parcel". Was any thought given to her concerns or misgivings?

— CHAPTER FOUR —

William Hancock, was born in 1853 in Cardiff. His parents were travellers who journeyed throughout South Wales seeking work at fair or fete. It was whilst they were journeying through Glamorgan that William's father died. He is buried at Llanblethian near Cowbridge, a pleasant town a few miles from Cardiff.

As adults, the three Hancock siblings continued the family's travelling traditions, eventually owning the financially successful W.C. & S. Hancock Empire.

By the late 1870s, William, always one step ahead of his competitors, took a huge financial risk and made capital investments in steam powered engines, improving the efficiency of transporting equipment from town to town and increasing the family's collective fortunes even further. He and his wife Mrs Sophie, (who was born in Southampton), had settled in Plymouth some years previously. Unswerving loyalty to his extended family, who were integral to the success of his business, ensured they would always travel with him.

Every summer, under the keen eye of his sister Sophie, the modern steam-powered roundabouts were stowed aboard the wagons ready for travel. Their home at the Winter Gardens in Plymouth was shuttered up before they headed towards the north Devon town of Barnstaple. William and Charles encouraged every horse and driver to make safe passage over the wild and sparsely populated moorlands of the mid-Devonshire countryside. The demanding trek to Barnstaple, situated on the river Taw, passed isolated farmsteads tucked into brown bracken-covered hillsides. By the turn of the century the Barnstaple Fair had become a premier event across the country. And William Hancock had played no small part in its success.

During the latter part of the 19th century Hancock had introduced his 4-abreast Gallopers and a mechanised Joy Ride at the Fair, and in 1907 the introduction of the novelty Helter Skelter furthered his popularity. The family's involvement with the North Devon fair continued undiminished until 1913. An extraordinary event, however, then resulted in the downturn of their collective fortunes.

By the end of the Great War hostilities in 1918, the Hancocks had ceased to participate at the fair. Contemporary records refer to them as having suffered a major catastrophe during 1913.

Extensive news coverage appeared in the *Plymouth Press*, reporting the outcome of a serious fire. This fire coincided with the arrival, in Plymouth, of a group of Suffragettes in early December. These militant young women, bent on promoting the profile of their political movement, intensified the stakes of their demonstrations and marches, to an unlawful act of fire razing, destroying a timber yard at Richmond Walk. Although there was no mention of their intended target, once ignited the fire spread rapidly before blazing out of control, raging towards the open ground nearby, where the Hancocks' fantastic "World Fair" equipment was stored. The intensity of the flames caused considerable damage. The loss of several prime carousels and roundabouts including the fabulously decorated facades and specialist equipment were burnt beyond recognition. Restoration was impossible; not one of these iconic pieces was to be salvaged. The losses were irreplaceable. It was a devastating blow to the family, who were already experiencing dwindling popularity. There was yet more disastrous news to follow when a further outcome of the catastrophe became apparent. Sympathetic gossip spread amongst other travellers as rapidly as the destructive fire. The family, it was confided, had no insurance. The Hancocks were ruined.

However, between 1889 and 1900, prior to the Great War and the fire that was to affect their future appearances at Barnstaple, William and Mrs Sophie thrived.

He would often recall the many years of experience in a circus environment. How, after his father died whilst working near Cowbridge, he and his mother continued to travel with other fairground operators, one of which was the famous Chipperfields Circus. When just twelve years old, he was responsible for pushing a little roundabout around with his hand. It was all they had after the death of his father Richard, yet he reflected how grateful he was for these earlier experiences, enabling him to establish his own travelling entertainment business at a young age.

William enjoyed the commendations of his fellow travellers. He was described by many as "a master showman who could get in touch with the people" and "an uncut diamond with a heart of gold". His adaptability and forward thinking anticipated the need for modernisation and he made the transition to mechanisation early in his career, one of the first showmen to do so when he introduced steam-powered roundabouts at his funfair. These modern innovations fulfilled William's prediction, and William, Charles and Miss Sophie Hancock became beneficiaries of their status as the most famous Circus and Fairground proprietors associated with the West Country during the Victorian and early Edwardian periods.

Miss Sophie, who never married, was regarded by the travelling community as a woman who "stood her ground in the rough world of travelling"; in appearance having "a face like a road map printed on leather" with "the loudest voice at any fair", a fairground character recognised also by her love of outrageous hats.

The blood of an entrepreneur flowed through William Hancock's veins. His showmanship guaranteed memorable fetes and galas often organised as part of a fundraising event.

His name alone ensured financial success. A Victorian benefactor and philanthropist, he would make generous contributions from his own profits to help boost the public donations, raising funds for hospitals and similar public institutions throughout the West Country.

*

Towards the middle of March, the Hancock entourage, together with their two nieces Henrietta and Harriet Henderson, had completed their trek from Devon to Bristol. William and his wife had no children of their own, Henrietta and Harriet having taken on the mantel of the Hancock's young family a few years previously. These two young women looked forward to Louie's arrival. Their warm welcome softened any anxieties Louie may have had. She was absorbed into this close knit environment, travelling with them to the many fairs and fetes. Whilst she was expected to carry out light domestic duties and act as companion to Mrs Sophie, these responsibilities were not too onerous, and left Louie with time to investigate and enjoy this new, exciting world.

Travelling around the country with an extensive train of wagons and "Iron horses" – the 1890s modern mechanised steam engines – was a slow, sometimes hazardous process. Country lanes, narrow and muddied could disrupt the passage of these lumbering, heavy vehicles, and accidents were not infrequent.

To ensure they arrived at the designated venue safely and in good time the colourful entourage had left their home in the Devonshire docks town and Naval Port of Plymouth towards the middle of March. William calculated that their journey to Bristol would cover 120 or so miles. This, he anticipated, would take several days and it would be important to preserve the good humour of family, personnel, the troupe, the wellbeing of the horses and to minimise the restlessness of the menagerie. The safety and health of these caged animals was essential to the fair, an important exhibit of wild beasts. If all went to plan the fair, bioscope and menagerie would be set up in Bristol by the end of the third week in March.

Horse-drawn vehicles led the cavalcade from the centre of Plymouth, passed the old Quay and the city's historic Barbican where trading ships from around the world were tied alongside, filling every mooring of the old Sutton harbour-side. The 18th century citadel gazed out over the Hoe towards the distant breakwater, hidden beneath an early morning mist, as the wagons made steady progress east towards Exeter. They crossed the old bridge over the River Plym and climbed the immediate hill in convoy towards the village communities of Ashburton and South Brent. They travelled through landscapes of soft red earth. Farmsteads dotted the rolling Devon hills, where flocks of sheep and fine dairy herds grazed, nourished by the fertile pastures. The approach to the Elizabethan town of Totnes – overlooked by the 12th century castle ruins – was a welcome sight after hours of travel through narrow, undulating country lanes. Here, the weary travellers and tired horses could rest for the night.

The route from Totnes the next morning criss-crossed the countryside towards the ancient seaport of Brixham and the seaside towns of Paignton and Torquay. Neither of these had yet been established as popular holiday destinations, although taking in the sea air for the benefit of both health and relaxation had become fashionable amongst the

Victorian middle classes.

Navigating the old roads towards the trading port of Exeter and the manufacturing market town of Bridgwater demanded yet more tiresome days of travel, but finally their destination appeared on the horizon. Once they arrived in Bristol, the teams of itinerant workers and casual labourers who regularly travelled around the showgrounds in search of work, set about unloading the vehicles and erecting the roundabouts, marquees, menagerie and bioscope. Their experience and efficiency ensured the showground would be ready to open for business the following day.

Into this heady mix of kaleidoscopic excitement arrived a young woman who could find all the adventure she was seeking.

— CHAPTER FIVE —

Contemporary correspondence written to the Crinks during early 1896 suggests they had moved from the terraced house in Queen Anne Road, to Beese's Tea Rooms in Conham, leaving behind the industrial suburbs of Barton hill for countryside on the outskirts of Bristol. It is not known whether they were employed at the tea rooms or were renting rooms as a family, initially with Louie. Historical records indicate she lived at Beese's Tea Rooms during the latter part of 1895, although there is no information as to whether she was still employed at Todd's Cloth factory in Bristol. What we do know is that by the spring of 1896 she was working and travelling with the Hancock family. It remains a mystery as to why William and Mary Crink moved to Conham but perhaps explains why Louie was given to Hancocks at that time.

Founded in 1848 by Ann Beese, the tea rooms remained inthe same family for many years. Thomas and Hannah Beese took over ownership in 1851 until the reins were handed on several years later to their closest relative George and his wife Caroline. Whilst trying to establish a connection between Mary Crinks and the Beese family, research showed that Mary had a sister, Caroline.

However, further investigation confirmed that Caroline Beese was not after all related to Mary; the possibility of a family connection was short lived. Caroline managed the tea rooms whilst "Captain George" ferried visitors across the river. The ferry was the only access at that time to the café and refreshments. The couple ran Beese's tea rooms together until the sudden death of George in 1895.

It was soon after George's demise that the Crinks moved to Conham.

Despite the death of her husband, Caroline continued to run the café assisted by one of her seven daughters.

It was essential to find an experienced ferryman, as without the regular crossing of the ferryboat there would be no customers, no trade and no livelihood. Gilbert Bruton, a young relative, was eventually employed as the new ferryman and continued to deliver passengers safely across the river to Beese's landing stage for many years. The site overlooked the reaches of the River Avon which flowed between a floating dock and Hanham, a happy union of river and the Kennet and Avon canal, the navigation of which was owned by the Great Western Railway.

It was a popular haunt with boat crews and labourers laying the tracks for Brunel's latest project (a railway line running from this industrial area towards Bristol), and workers from the busy industrial factories that lined the banks of the canal. This area, originally landscaped with wooded tranquillity, became heavily industrialised in the late 18th century and scarred the woodlands from nearby

Troopers Hill to Hanham Lock. In the early 19th century the riverbank was dominated by colliery wharves, the old stone quarry and early Victorian brass works. All of which polluted the countryside with smoke, noise and river traffic.

Business was brisk on this industrial waterway. Inland Navigation Companies plied their trade along the busy stretch of the Kennet and Avon Canal, navigating from Reading in Berkshire, via Bradford on Avon and Keynsham, to the docks at Hanham Lock.

Barges filled with local commodities, coal, brass and walling stones from the quarry at Troopers Hill, chugged through the bends and gentle curves of the Avon River, eventually off-loading their cargoes on the vast wharves in Berkshire, Wiltshire and Somerset.

So, what happened to Louie? There can be little doubt that she lived briefly with the Crinks at the riverside tea rooms in early 1896. Their plans for Louie to work for the Hancocks seemed to coincide with their arrival at the tea rooms, so we can assume she had left the factory soon after.

William Hancock's agreement to employ Louie in the spring of 1896 was a timely blessing for the Crinks as they settled in at Conham. If she was consulted, would she have been given an option to agree or disagree? However, it's unlikely that her opinion was considered relevant. And so Louie took up her position as companion and domestic help to Hancock's wife Sophie, when the Fair left Bristol in March a few weeks before Easter. The wagons and caravans were due to retrace their route from Bristol to Exeter in time for the Easter festivities.

However, they had an engagement in the market town of Taunton, before any thought of their Easter engagement could be fulfilled. Packing up the vast array of mechanical funfair equipment would require an army of helpers: artistes, animal tamers, fairground workers skilled and unskilled.

The menagerie, lions, tiger, bear and monkey had to be caged; mechanised rides dismantled and steam-powered traction engines attached; horse-drawn living caravans secured; the Rococo and Baroque carved and painted Bioscope façade carefully stowed; gallopers, gondolas, switchback rides safely stored. An imminent departure heralded by spurts of steam from traction engines, their ornate brass fitments gleaming. The rattle of iron rimmed wheels over cobbled roads in competition as wagons finally trundled out bound for the next town or city. The vast Hancock entourage left Bristol towards the end of March, en route to Taunton, a Somerset market town fifty miles from Bristol.

They travelled through countryside, villages and scattered farmsteads, the convoy welcomed by villagers from open cottage doors as they trundled by; animated children ran beside the lumbering wagons and horse-drawn caravans, agog at the spectacle. Handbills would be distributed and colourful posters pasted on trees, posts or farm gates, as the slow deliberate passage of vehicles drew ever nearer to their intended destination.

This became the day to day routine for Louie: exciting, transient and fascinating. Could she have ever imagined such a transition?

Louie's perception of Victorian Bristol was shaped by the life she had lead for fourteen years in drab industrial Barton Hill, a narrow terrace and back to back houses hastily built over marshland and cultivated farmland. In the mid-19th century, the open lands had been swept away in a frenzy of construction during rapid industrialisation. Demolition of 17th century stone farm cottages and old manor houses changed rural identities forever, displacing communities of farm workers and their country practices. Clusters of new dwellings created new neighbourhoods. The need for housing became paramount, large swathes of farmland were acquired, and ancient landmarks became casualties of urbanisation.

Housing was erected close to the factories; The Wagon Works, The Tannery, The Pottery and The Great Western Cotton Mill, another example of Brunel's industrial dominance. Each would employ hundreds of labourers who arrived from other impoverished parishes in search of employment. These workers, with their families in tow, converged on the Barton Hill district, filling the recently built terraces of back-to-back properties.

The Parish councils were under pressure to provide basic facilities for these needy migrants. Overcrowded residential areas could be a catalyst for disease.

A smallpox hospital had been erected in Barton Hill in the 19th century, as cholera had been rife in the middle of the 1800s and the authorities were anxious to prevent any such outbreaks happening again.

Education on the rudiments of public health was regarded as an imperative; once these migrant families were housed, education for their children was the next priority.

The Universal Education Act established in 1870 elected School Boards who had the power to enforce compulsory attendance of children between the ages of five and twelve years. Responsibility for the provision of educational opportunities fell squarely on the shoulders of the ratepayers of each Poor Law Union. They were charged to monitor all such facilities within their area.

With the influx of so many young children, a commitment for extra schools to accommodate infants and juniors, girls and boys was essential. The minimum school-leaving age was raised from eleven to twelve years. Then the revised Act of 1876 stated no child could be employed between ten and fourteen years of age unless a Labour Certificate had been issued. This was determined when each child had reached the necessary educational standard. They had to attain competence to "Standard 1V" (Reading, Writing and Arithmetic) or receive a certificate confirming a minimum attendance figure of 250 days, before a Labour Certificate could be issued. In most cases girls and boys remained at school until they were thirteen or fourteen years of age. Louie would have conformed to these educational standards. She had gained her labour certificate in the summer of 1895.

To address the shortage of schools, additional land was hastily acquired. Unfortunately in many cases it was close to factories, railway lines, industrial depots and overcrowded housing. School buildings were hurriedly designed and erected.

There were also an impressive number of public houses in the area of Barton Hill, catering for the abiding thirsts and social interaction amongst the local residents: The Royal Exchange, Locomotive Tavern, The Gardeners Arms and the Rhubarb Tavern, to name but a few.

The Rhubarb Tavern was built on the site of the old 17th century Queen Anne's House, an historical link preserved in the naming of Queen Anne Road. Named after the abundance of rhubarb fields that once covered this area of rural tranquillity, until the 1830s when houses began to sprout up all over the once fertile soil. The Rhubarb Tavern is the oldest building to survive to the 21st century. A building now in isolation, the Victorian remnants hidden by a modern red brick façade. Flower baskets hang from the frontage and a row of small 19th century houses nudge the walls of the public house, built on the site of an old pottery factory.

Queen Anne Road would have been enriched then, by neighbourly chatter and children playing nearby as trains rattled past pell-mell heading towards the centre of Bristol.

Spiritual needs were taken into consideration too. The church of St. Luke, the Mission House Sunday school, the Medical Mission, the Christian Cottage Mission and the Factory Street Mission all administered to the residents' bodily, temporal and spiritual welfare.

This would have been Louie's world: noisy streets filled with smoke from factories and chimney-stacks; the lamplighter's early morning shouts, gas lighting pole clattering against windows to wake the lie-a-beds; clogs pounding the cobbles, familiar and secure.

She was educated at the school in Queen Anne Road, a short walk away from her home. The grey stone lintels of the building were set into porches giant-high, with identities carved deep in old stone; girls one side, boys the other.

Wooden desks and black writing slates filled the classrooms. Childish laughter etched deep into each red brick; a memorable building to generations of children. (The building still stands but the gash-gaping windows are now steel shuttered.)

The Rhubarb Public House was a spit away from the school where local patrons moistened their throats and quenched thirsts whilst children swotted in classrooms or skipped and hopped in playgrounds.

Nearby St Luke's Church holds on to its precious island of green and pleasant land, whilst all around there is an ebb and flow of change. Where the ripening stalks of rhubarb once flourished, where fields were ploughed and seed sown, now there's a garage, workshops and small family owned shops. To walk down Queen Anne Road today promotes memories of the past, although the narrow road once lined by terrace housing has been replaced by small modern residences.

At the time of the 1891 census, William, Mary and Louie, then ten years old, were still living in Queen Anne Road, Barton Hill.

In that same year, her mother, partner and their seven-year-old son Albert returned to live one street away, in Barton Hill Road. Was this a conscious decision to be near her daughter?

Despite living in such close proximity to Louie, Mary Ann did not take back ownership of her child. Mother and daughter continued to live apart.

Louie would remain with her adoptive parents for another four years. There was, however, a strong bond of affection between Louie and her half-brother Albert. They attended the same school in Queen Anne Road, and no doubt would have played together.

We can only imagine what Louie's understanding was of the arrangements made several years before. Did she wonder why her mother was living one street away whilst caring for another child? Did she feel resentment and rejection? Would they have considered the emotional impact on the young girl? Although Mary Ann seemed determined to remain in contact with Louie, what reasons did she give for not reclaiming her daughter?

Young Albert's love for his "big sister" was well documented. Had Mary Ann taken Louie back to live with them, how different might her daughter's life have been?

— CHAPTER SIX —

The continuous search for work was a constant worry for travellers. Whilst the Industrial Revolution created an upward surge in employment for many it seems unlikely that William and Mary Crinks would have benefitted from this. Their background in funfairs and theatre had not equipped them for the rapid march of industrialisation.

As mentioned, during the 1870s Mary had been living and working in Pontypool, a few miles north of Newport in South Wales with her first husband, Albert Baker and their young son Stephen. Their mutual affection for Victorian theatricals brought them together, and as we know Mary's family was a fascinating group of performers who worked and travelled with circuses and funfairs for many years. Her sister, Caroline Butcher, was an acknowledged professional tightrope walker of renown in the 1860s, and her Great Aunt Lizzie found fame as a lion tamer. Mary's choice of career as an actress was also unconventional, and as mentioned previously she trod the boards as an actress with a West Country touring ensemble: Bakers Portable Theatre Company.

Whilst these artistes were not blood relations of Louie, their exotic lifestyles may have influenced her secret ambitions. She would no doubt have heard stories of their adventures and may have known Mary's sister, Caroline.

Louie had appeared in theatrical productions when just a young girl, most notably, cast in the role of Willie Carlisle, a popular stage classic of the time *East Lynne*, adapted and dramatised from a novelette by Victorian author Ellen Wood.

The ageing William Crinks referred frequently to his friendship with the Studts family from Swansea, who were circus and travelling funfair owners (and would provide the Old Welsh Fair at The Fine Arts Exhibition in Cardiff). His close friendship with the Hancocks family provided William with several opportunities for itinerant work over the years, a close-knit community who helped and supported one another. Louie felt safe amongst these hard-working but caring folk.

Travelling throughout the West Country would not have been a novelty, although living in caravans away from her home city of Bristol would be a very different experience. She would no longer be living near her birth mother, or able to meet with her dear friend Louisa Honeyfield nor her half-brother. There was little time for sentiment or adjustment. When the Hancock entourage packed up and left Bristol, Louie was expected to adapt to her new life quickly as a young woman with the opportunity to grow in confidence and achieve her ambitions away from the protective cloak of her adoptive parents.

By the time Hancock's fair, menagerie and Bioscope had arrived and set up in the market square of Taunton, Louie had settled in as one of these travellers.

Taunton was, at that time, a Victorian small market town whose growth had expanded from a Saxon village to a 10th century town with a population of a few hundred. The original fortified settlement surrounded by ditch and rampart boasted a thriving mint and a busy market. Famous in the 13th century for its wool industry this local product found favour in Europe and Africa. By the 19th century, industrialisation had arrived, challenging the town's inhabitants to embrace the future. Taunton rose to the challenge and became renowned for brewing, and iron founding.

With the promise of spring chivvying the reluctant from cottage fireside and homestead hearth, the people of Taunton and the surrounding countryside villages were eager to enjoy the travelling fairs and fetes, and anxious to spend their hard-earned pennies. Mechanical rides, swing boats, coconut shies and exotic food displays all vied invitingly for their custom.

A week or so after the Hancocks' departure from Bristol, William Crinks undertook a journey from the tea gardens at Conham to the fairground site in Taunton. William Hancock deemed it essential to have all the entertainment equipment overhauled ahead of the Exeter Easter Fair and William Crinks was just the man to gild and paint the famous "Gallopers" and other crowd-pleasing roundabouts. Each horse was a triumph of his artistic talents. Blues, reds, yellow and golden brilliance bounced off the whirling roundabouts. At completion of the work, hands were shaken, cash changed hands, goodbyes were said, and perhaps a last hug given to Louie. Did he turn around to wave one last time, or call out goodbye to her as he set off?

When questioned four months later, he would confirm that "his Louie" seemed settled with the Hancock family. But would he have realised otherwise? Mary Ann Evans sent a message to her daughter seeking reassurance that her dear girl was happy in her new environment. Although she would express her doubts later, complaining how much she missed seeing Louie.

With the equipment spruced up and packed, the Hancock troupe travelled the twenty or so miles south west, reaching Exeter by April 5th in time for the Easter festivities. There is no record of how long they remained in Exeter, and nothing more is recorded about the Hancocks or Louie until the fair, menagerie and Bioscope arrived in Cornwall six weeks later.

As they passed through Devon, en route to their next engagement William Hancock may have taken the opportunity to return to his home base at Market Place in Plymouth. In the 1890s, William rented a section of the disused sugar refinery, a building that dominated the centre of Plymouth and acted as a convenient location in which to store his fairground equipment and menagerie during the winter months. The premises also provided an opportunity to repair or exchange any damaged equipment in readiness for their journey further south towards their Cornish destinations.

They arrived in Redruth at the beginning of June. This Cornish town had experienced fluctuating industrial fortunes and misfortunes during the previous one hundred years, the marks of which were borne stoically by the town and its' inhabitants. Hard times could be forgotten as the great iron horses of Hancock's fair were welcomed, making their slow, ponderous progress down the high street, towards the town's recreation ground.

Weeks of anticipation by local residents had prepared everyone to welcome the invasion of the glamorous travelling showmen. Crowds gathered in the High Street long before the colourful cavalcade rumbled into town. Children in Sunday best jigged back and forth, eager to be first to catch sight of these people from another world. Flags and bunting decorated the streets, and fluttered from every lamppost, appearing overnight as if by the wave of a magic wand. Excitement was without parallel as this year in 1896, Redruth would witness an entertainment not seen previously in Cornwall.

Despite such overt displays of excitement and acclamation, rumours circulated amongst the travelling community suggested traditional fairs with traditional entertainers were failing to attract the crowds. The novelty of steam driven roundabouts, acrobats, so-called freak shows, stalls and wild animals was beginning to wane, a worry for the many owners, showmen and their troupes of performers.

The family discussed the impact this could have on their business. Always ahead of the game, William and Charles, with their sister Sophie's approval, announced, "We are introducing the art of the Aeronaut to our entertainments." Sensational, with elements of danger, this would surely re-capture audiences' interest throughout the West Country. The consequences of their decision would affect them all.

— CHAPTER SEVEN —

The aerial balloon displays exhibited during the late 19th century revitalised interest beyond the expectations of even the most optimistic of entrepreneurs. The idea excited the general public with the possibility of incident or disaster and added a frisson to the performance. The crowds demanded to see the latest phenomenon for themselves.

Demonstrations of aeronautical performances appeared first in London, drawing crowds back to the fairgrounds Balloonists had been risking limb, life and finances since the late 18th century. The first manned flight of a hot air balloon took place on 21st November 1783 from the Chateau le Muette, in Paris.

Brothers Joseph and Etienne Montgolfer's balloon made of paper and fuelled by a mixture of wool and straw, remained aloft for twenty-five minutes and travelled a distance of two miles before landing safely. Ten days later they successfully launched a gas balloon from the Tuillerie Gardens in Paris. The first recorded ascent in Britain took place nine months later in Edinburgh on 25th August in 1784 when James Tytler made a very short hop in a rudimentary hot air balloon. History does not record how high the hop was or how long it lasted. It does, however, tell us that Mr Tytler was lucky to survive.

James Sadler was more successful when he ascended in a hot air balloon from Oxford a few weeks later on 4th October. From these inauspicious beginnings the development of both gas-filled and hot air balloons developed rapidly. From 1784 until the early 1800s it would seem that the skies over Britain were alive with the sounds and sights of experimental balloons; their occupants in some instances a protest of cats, dogs and pigeons. Despite a superfluity of clothing it seems women were not deterred from participating either. In June 1784 a Mrs Sage, became the first Englishwoman to climb into a tiny basket and balloon into the sky, thus claiming the title of the First English Lady Aeronaut.

Throughout this period, designs of gas balloons improved as the evolution of an approximately spherical-shaped envelope of rubberised silk or similar material advanced.

Development of an open-ended neck allowed gas to escape as it expanded when changes of temperature and pressure occurred; a valve at the top of the balloon allowing the gas to be discharged at the will of the aeronaut.

During their early development, balloons were contained in a covering of netting at the bottom of which hung a horizontally mounted hoop. From beneath this a car or basket would be suspended. Ballast, usually sand, could be jettisoned during the flight causing the balloon to ascend The descent was achieved by the captain "valving the gas". Contemporary reports suggest bottles of brandy and wine were also jettisoned when sand failed to achieve the required height.

The complexity of balloon development and construction gathered pace in the years that followed. The flight of the first hot air balloon, fuelled by a mixture of wool and straw – the opening being held over a trench filled with combustible material – could take a day to inflate. This was superceded by gas-filled/hydrogen balloons (hydrogen or coal gas).

Charles Green experimented with coal gas in the early 1800s in an attempt to increase lifting power. It was cheaper, more readily available and preferred by Mr Green as an alternative to hydrogen. Free gas balloons (the gas being supplied by the local gas company) also became popular.

"Right-away" balloons incorporated a simple quick release mechanism. A parachute could be attached directly to the bottom of the envelope or basket using a cotter pin, thus allowing the aeronaut to detach and descend by parachute. The empty balloon could then free-fall into open countryside or, less conveniently, in to water.

Military Observation balloons were tethered to a steel winch and used as a civilian joy-riding craft for fee-paying passengers. The Observation balloon could rise to a height of 1,000 feet affording views of town and countryside hitherto unseen by the public. It would then be hauled back to earth, disgorging the thrill-seekers safely. These balloons were also used for progressive scientific research.

Ballooning arrived comparatively late in South Wales due to the dominance of agriculture. The estimated population of Cardiff in 1801 was 1,870. Eighty years later, due to industrial demands for exports of coal and iron, the population had risen to over 100,000.

However, despite the local populous being less than 2,000 at the beginning of the 19th century, the residents in the surrounding towns and villages responded enthusiastically to rumours of an exciting event and turned out in force when the first attempt at flight by a Francis Barratt was due to take place at Swansea on 6th October 1802. By eight o'clock a crowd of some 8,000 had arrived to watch from the designated launch site. Hundreds more gathered elsewhere in fields, hills and on ships at anchor in the nearby harbour. After several unsuccessful attempts to take off and with a near riot imminent, the crowd were eventually subdued by the promise of another attempt.

Nine days later, on the 15th October at precisely four o'clock, with a triumphant Mr Barratt on board, the balloon finally rose to a height of sixty feet. Although, not before he had jettisoned ballast and a large leg of mutton, stowed away should he be airborne for a prolonged period. On this second attempt he sailed away only to land in a row of trees. The crowd became ever more restless and after several unsuccessful attempts the balloon launched once again, at which point Barratt jumped from the basket as it sailed up, up and away. When found later by two farmhands, crumpled beyond repair at the point of impact, they decided to share the gift from above and cut the balloon in half.

Balloons of varying size continued to carry their occupants on unpredictable voyages, some for a few miles, others depositing their occupants far from civilisation after many hours of uncontrolled flight. In the summer of 1844 a balloonist of unknown identity, launched from Cardiff. A northerly wind quickly carried him over the Bristol Channel Neither the balloon nor occupant were seen or heard of again.

In November 1881 Newport-born Mr Walter Powell, MP for Malmesbury, made "a sensational ascent from Cardiff in Daystar". He landed safely several miles away near Cirencester.

However, a month later he was not so fortunate. He launched from the city of Bath in "Saladin", sailed in the direction of the English Channel and disappeared without trace; one balloon adventure too many for Malmesbury's parliamentary representative.

During many subsequent attempts by these pioneers, several articles of clothing, at least one barometer and vast amounts of sand were jettisoned. A Mr R. Green holds the unlikely distinction of jettisoning a cat, much against its will, tied up in a net and attached to a parachute. Apparently the cat landed in a vessel tied alongside Cardiff's Bute Dock, shaken but unhurt.

The same cannot be said of Mr Green who vacated the balloon as it descended at Sand Point near Clevedon in Somerset, and vanished without trace. The fate of the balloon was much less dramatic; it was found later in a field near Wedmore in Somerset.

During the late 19th century balloon flights from Pleasure Gardens in London became a regular and popular feature. Several attempts to secure records for the longest and furthest flights took place from the spectacular Vauxhall Pleasure Gardens. Launches also took place from the Crystal Palace, the Alexandra Gardens and Lords cricket ground.

When a Mr Glaisher made several scientific ascents he declared afterwards he had seen "meteorological phenomena". Ballooning was evolving.

As the sport became appreciably more reliable, and safety improved for participant and observer, Victorian entrepreneurs saw the potential for ballooning as a new show business initiative: "there was money to be made."

Balloonists soon enjoyed the trappings of fame, becoming the feted celebrities of their day: parachuting balloonists, the public's must-see event. Greater control of the parachute was achieved towards the end of the 19th century with an improvement in design. Engineers introduced a mushroom shaped canopy of silken material (similar to that used today). Unlike today's parachutes it hung from the balloon and was not stowed in packs or attached to the parachutist by a harness. However, the improved design did not aid control over direction. Steering was ineffectual; achieved by hauling on the rigging lines to dispel air from the parachute's canopy.

A trapeze bar was attached to rigging lines beneath the balloon, from which a webbing sling was suspended where the aeronaut would sit. Prior to flight most would have attached themselves to the trapeze bar by a lanyard sporting quick release clips. The more foolhardy dispensed with this safety harness and relied solely on gripping the bar with their hands.

Many of the aeronauts were from circus backgrounds. Several were young women, an added attraction, all of whom adopted exotic pseudonyms and wore flamboyant costumes which caused a degree of controversy.

People flocked to venues where an aeronaut was appearing and popularity of this attraction continued until the outbreak of World War I. During the 19th century and early 20th century, displays by balloonists and parachutists abounded. One of the most popular exponents was Auguste

Eugene Gaudron, a dapper French professional balloonist who had made ascents and descents throughout Europe and Britain. Attractive and debonair, he was a daring and charismatic performer. He would make many epic balloon flights during his lifetime, some of which would cross the English Channel to Europe and Scandinavia. He also would make the first manned airmail flight from Britain to Calais.

In 1891 he married Marina Spencer, the daughter of Percival Spencer, owner of the prestigious balloon manufacturing and operating company "Spencer & Sons of London" (founded by pioneer Charles Green Spencer in early 1800s). This proved very beneficial for the ambitious Frenchman and his future plans.

By the turn of the century Spencer & Sons and their famous brother-in-law Auguste Gaudron had acquired near monopoly of British civil aeronautics. He invested in his own company and built up a successful business "Alexandra Park Aviation Works" at Duke's Avenue in Muswell Hill.

His fame and fortune increased with his many epic and unconventional flights throughout Britain and the Continent, in one instance landing on Russian soil.

His decision to employ female assistants whilst pleasing the crowds was looked on with disapproval amongst elements of Victorian society. One of these exotic young lady balloonists who performed with Gaudron was Miss Alma Beaumont. In the spring of 1896 the duo were contracted to join William Hancock for a season of fairs, fetes and galas throughout the West Country. Gaudron and Alma Beaumont joined the Hancocks as the entourage made its slow progress towards Cornwall, in preparation for their aerial displays of derring-do.

The final performers in this story had made their timely entrance.

— CHAPTER EIGHT —

In early June, William Hancock, his family and of course Louie left Plymouth behind, crossed over the New Bridge into Cornwall at Gunnislake and headed south towards the mining town of Redruth.

They had arrived well in advance of their engagement. The important date in their calendar, and the town's too, was June 17th. Advertised in Redruth's local press as a "Monstre Fete and Gala" (sic) "The largest and grandest outside London, under most Distinguished Patronage". The Grand Fete and Gala, sponsored by William Hancock, was to be held at the Recreation Ground in aid of the Miners Hospital and also West Cornwall Women's Hospital. The local press referred to Messrs Hancock as "always to the fore where enterprise is concerned".

At midday a procession commencing from the ancient hilltop landmark Carn Brea, rising one mile south west of Redruth, announced the start of the day's activities.

Participants gathered in readiness to process through the town. The streets were bedecked with bunting and brightly coloured flags fluttered from open windows. The lengthy procession, led by vehicles of Redruth and Cambourne fire brigades, were accompanied by ten bands and several cyclists, both ladies and gentlemen, who were eager to participate in the cycling races planned for later that day. A cycle track had been erected at the recreation ground especially for the purpose.

The ground itself was ablaze with colour and music. Mechanical bright-painted figures twirled and turned to the sounds of brash organ music; warmth flooded out from the hundreds of electric lights surrounding Hancock's roundabouts, swings, side shows and stalls. Crowds of fare-paying customers were transported by miniature train through the "Channel Tunnel from Dover to Calais" (in anticipation of Eurostar many years later perhaps). Others enjoyed the "canals of Venice" in stylish gondolas.

At dusk a grand display of fireworks "with magnificent new Mechanical Devices" delighted crowds. However, prior to the firework display, "The Event of the day", would be the balloon ascent by Madame Alma Beaumont. Anticipation amongst the twenty thousand visitors who milled around the recreation ground and funfair built as they eagerly awaited the talented Miss Beaumont. It would be her first appearance in the West Country.

Zalva and his high wire troupe had performed marvellous acts on high ladders, and athletic movements on horizontal bars which were enjoyed immensely during the day. But, it was universally agreed the event favoured above all others, was the balloon ascent by Madame Alma Beaumont.

Her flight was recorded in the local press as "a little lady who made a truly grand ascent and descended with the aid of her parachute. After ascending to a height of between 3,000 and 4,000 feet she detached herself from the balloon, and fell swiftly for some distance; but the parachute almost immediately opened out, and the parachutist floated away eastward, and dropped about a mile from the starting point".

When Alma made her reappearance "after her dangerous exploit" she was feted handsomely on her successful landing. The crowd, who a short time before had applauded her ascent, cheered heartily as the diminutive aeronaut walked through the recreation ground towards her caravan.

The adventurous Madame Alma Beaumont made her first professional balloon flight aged twenty-one with Spencer & Sons in 1891. She soon became an integral part of this internationally famous company. She gained fame and popularity previously as a professional swimmer, starring in "Captain Roytons Water Show", until changing the direction of her career. She remained at the forefront of the Spencer Brothers' business, appearing most frequently with Auguste Gaudron. They toured the country together from 1891 until July 1896. Alma made at least thirty-five recorded descents and many hundreds of ascents from gas-filled balloons, over the five year period.

An epic flight undertaken by Miss Beaumont on 24th June from Glasgow was a near disaster very early in her career. According to a contemporary report, after ascending through rain clouds the parachute had become so wet that when she prepared to descend she considered the 'chute to be useless. She made a brave decision to remain with the balloon, doing so until the gas-filled sphere finally landed, astonishingly sustaining only a few bruises. Despite this traumatic experience Alma remained an aeronaut, gaining plaudits as a "plucky little lady".

So what had happened to Louie? By the time the travellers had arrived at Redruth in Cornwall, it would seem she had settled in well. Since leaving Bristol her travels had taken her through familiar countryside and villages en route to Taunton, Exeter and Plymouth: the itinerant lifestyle she had known as a young child.

She found friendship with Henrietta and Harriett, Mrs Sophie's nieces and her light domestic duties allowed her free time to watch many of the artistes perform. She became acquainted with several of the artistes, one of whom, Zalva the American high wire performer, paid particular attention to her. It was the balloonists and parachutists, however, that captivated Louie. Although the young girl did not understand the complexity of the procedures necessary to ensure successful flights, she became totally fascinated, and completely absorbed by this exciting phenomenon.

Professional preparation and thorough safety checks of the equipment were dependent on experienced operators and their assistants Preparation in readiness for late afternoon or early evening launches would continue throughout the day; balloons and parachutes examined for rips or tears caused during previous flights by a small army of dedicated assistants

Different systems for filling the envelope were used over the years, resulting in several fatalities.

Professional balloonists were anxious to find a system and it was agreed the most efficient and safest way was to fill the envelope with gas from a local gas pipe outlet. However, approval and permission from town or city officials would have to be sought.

If approved, the gas outlet was then relayed to the inert balloon spread out in readiness for the launch. The quantity of gas needed was calculated by the capacity of the balloon. This would determine the height to which it could safely ascend. Frenchman

Auguste Gaudron favoured balloons containing 20,000 cubic metres when inflated, as his flights often reached a height of 8,000 feet or more.

The balloon in which Alma planned to ascend on the 17th June contained 13,000 cubic metres and could ascend to approximately 5,000 feet.

Whilst early morning ascents were preferred by some balloonists, late afternoon or early evening flights were deemed the safest as prevailing wind conditions were considered to be less unpredictable.

By the middle of June, the Hancock entourage, Auguste Gaudron and Miss Beaumont had reached a mutually agreeable routine. They would share the aerial performances over the town of Redruth. And Louie became acquainted with the Frenchman.

It was during one of his visits to William Hancock's private caravan complex at the recreation ground that Gaudron met her for the first time. He would later make reference to the meeting, describing her as a pleasant young woman, believing her to be about eighteen years of age. Although he recalled the meeting as "unmemorable" at the time. Whilst this event may have been trivial to him, to Louie this initial introduction to the French aeronaut sparked a surprising and bold response. Perhaps in an attempt to be noticed by him, she suggested that she could look after the balloon and parachute equipment at the completion of each flight. Her daily chores for Sophie Hancock were not too onerous, she confided, and, if he agreed, she could easily find time to guard the wagon with the precious equipment. Vast crowds milled around the launch sites and landing grounds, and ever mindful of the safety of the expensive equipment and costs associated with any damage, Gaudron decided to accept her offer. She could keep an eye on the wagon and its contents once the balloon and parachute had been retrieved and returned to the Hancock's private enclosure. She had become intrigued by the flight preparation processes and watched every one of the performances by Auguste Gaudron and Alma Beaumont with increasing interest.

However, a curious and unexplained occurrence took place during their first meeting. She introduced herself to Gaudron as Grace Parry (identified later as the name of Mary Crinks' niece and no relation to Louie). Whilst working for the Hancocks, Louie received several letters. Addressed not to Louie Crinks, but to Miss Grace Parry C/o W. Hancock, and postmarked Bristol. It was established during research that these letters came from the Crinks. Seemingly it was their decision to initiate the deception. If, as seems probable, these letters were delivered directly to William and Sophie Hancock, were they also aware of the deception? Or had they been deceived too? Did the Crinks introduce "their Louie" to William and Mrs Sophie as their niece Grace Parry? What, one wonders, could have been the reason for such a deception?

And both M. Gaudron and Miss Beaumont believed her name was Grace Parry.

This unexplained deception could so easily have been discovered. Perhaps it was simply a whim of Louie's choosing. Or were the Crinks still determined to conceal the girl's connection to her birth mother? Concerned the truth would expose Mary Ann, living in Bristol with her partner and their illegitimate son Albert?

Why the Crinks, Louie and possibly the Hancocks all chose to perpetuate the deception remains an unresolved mystery.

Whilst looking after the rescued balloons Louie came into frequent contact with the aeronauts and the enthusiasm with which she guarded the wagon and its contents was obvious for everyone to see. Miss Beaumont and M. Gaudron alternated their flights, ascending into the skies far above the old tin and copper mining town of Redruth, although by the time of the Hancocks visit most of the mines had closed. However there remained a cluster of derelict chimney stacks and old engine housings which were potential hazards for the parachutists. Amongst the crowds who watched these ascents was this young girl who observed every preparation before each of the flights. She witnessed the crowd's excitement as Alma walked towards the inflated balloon; observed the glamorous costume worn by Alma, her peaked sailor cap clinging precariously to her long curls.

The girl noticed how the gas-filled balloon swayed above so many heads, all upturned in anticipation for its lift-off, the seat of webbing hanging below the pear drop canopy, held safe by the tethering lines until such time as Alma or Gaudron would take their position on the narrow webbing seat. She observed how the aeronauts, after gripping the balloon's wooden hoop and clipping the safety lanyard to the harness, would nod to their team to release the retaining ropes and after a moment's hesitation, the balloon would begin to climb. At first it would rise slowly, before gathering speed as it rose to a height of some 6,000 to 8,000 feet, the aeronaut a small, dark speck swinging beneath.

The parachute would hang loosely, attached to the centre of

the balloon by a thin, narrow cord. As the balloon reached the desired height, the aeronaut jumped from the webbing seat, the thin cord breaking away from the balloon, releasing the parachute. The parachutist could free-fall one hundred feet before the canopy inflated, trusting they would land in open countryside away from chimney stacks, trees, tall buildings and water.

Outwardly glamorous and exciting the inherent danger of an accident became very real. The history of ballooning was filled with fatalities. This activity was not for the faint hearted and not to be taken lightly by impressionable young women.

By the end of June the Hancock entourage had visited sites in Truro and Falmouth before making their return journey to Devon in time for their next engagement in the seaside town of Torquay.

Louie observed every launch, every ascent and descent. She watched each procedure beforehand and witnessed the cheering crowds and adulation experienced by Alma and Gaudron. She began to consider that this glamorous life could be her world too.

— CHAPTER NINE —

The grand opening of the anticipated "Fine Arts, Industrial and Maritime Exhibition" was due to take place on 2nd May 1896 at Cathays Park – a delightful, green oasis in the centre of the busy industrial town of Cardiff. The culmination of challenging committee meetings, unrealistic proposals, plans and disagreements, to the relief of the Exhibition Executive council.

The concept for this ambitious project had been initiated three years earlier in 1893, by public figures, local businessmen and industrialists. Designated the Exhibition Executive council they would oversee the organisation and running of the proposed Fine Arts exhibition. Their original plans were to open within one year in 1894. However, this was soon agreed as unrealistic and eventually an achievable date was agreed upon, opinion favouring the beginning of May 1896.

Their primary concern was to find suitable land in Cardiff as a venue for their enterprise and they were fortunate indeed when John Patrick, the 3rd Marquess of Bute, landowner and benefactor, offered them attractive parkland in the centre of the town.

The association of the Bute family with the town of Cardiff had existed for many years. This relationship was beneficial for both the town and the Butes. The Aristocratic Scottish Lord, John Stuart was considered fortuitous in his marriage to Charlotte Jane Windsor in 1766 as Charlotte was heiress to the historic Cardiff Castle, the surrounding grounds and 11,000 acres of land throughout South Wales. John Stuart took the title of 1st Marquess of Bute, acquired estates in Scotland and became custodian of vast tracts of land throughout Cardiff and the County of Glamorgan. The Bute family continued to maintain their involvement with the town for a further 200 years.

Their canny financial investments in the building of the Bute Docks and early 19th century railway systems were to make Cardiff one of the busiest ports in the world during its heyday in the 19th and 20th centuries.

The Castle stands now at the southern end of NorthRoad where the North Gate and Old Town Wall once stood.

Transformed, by the time of the Fine Arts Exhibition in 1896, into a neo-Gothic fantasy by the visionary Victorian architect William Burges.

Fifty acres of cultivated land owned by John Patrick, the 3rd Marquess, lay to the east of the castle and it was this prime site with avenues of mature trees, shrubs and established pathways that he offered to the Exhibition Executive.

This was the perfect solution. The Executive Council agreed that the situation of Cathays Park, in the centre of the town, would do very nicely.

With the approach of Easter in early April and the Grand Opening due on May 2nd the Council were anxious to finalise their comprehensive exhibition plans. The building of a lake, canal, concert hall, art museum, Indian bazaar and a mine were but a few of the elaborate projects that had to be completed before the Grand Opening.

Discussions about the logistics of this ambitious event and its affect on the town dominated their meetings. They were determined at the outset that their vision for a Fine Arts, Industrial and Maritime Exhibition would encompass both educational and recreational opportunities. Their priority was to support development of the many natural resources and manufacturing process in South Wales, to increase the prosperity and happiness of its people and to establish a fund for the benefit of public institutions within the town. Their "Record of Intent" faithfully recorded in the town's council minutes.

Such a prestigious event would benefit from receiving royal approval and to everyone's delight the royal nod had been given. The exhibition would come under the patronage of Her Majesty Queen Victoria. Although the Prince of Wales and his wife Princess Alexandra would not be able to officiate at the Grand Opening Ceremony on the 2nd

May, they would, however, visit Cardiff and the exhibition a few weeks later towards the end of June.

Filmmaking was in its infancy at this time, so it was something of a coup when American-born moviemaker Birt

Acres planned to film the visit of the Prince of Wales. It would be a historic milestone in filmmaking; the first film to be made and exhibited to a public audience in Wales. A few months before, in early April, Mr. Acres had screened several films privately to the Cardiff Photographic Society, the "first projected cinema" to be shown in Wales, his achievement pre-empting the Lumiere Brothers "first" by a week. And it had taken place in the town of Cardiff.

The Rt. Hon. Lord Windsor, Lord Lieutenant of Glamorgan and Mayor of Cardiff had accepted the position of President of the Exhibition with enthusiasm.

Souvenirs of the Fine Arts exhibition were being produced in abundance, anticipating the thousands of visitors who it was hoped would visit the town.

Mr McClean, the MP for Cardiff was so inspired by the project as to suggest the Government should recognise Cardiff "as the metropolis of Wales".

The Grand Opening was to be preceded with a procession through all the principal streets by attending dignitaries. The town, the residents, shopkeepers, innkeepers, worthies and the less worthy were holding their collective breaths – the event anticipated by officials and public alike.

— CHAPTER TEN —

At the beginning of May Louisa, Gaudron, Alma and the Hancocks were many miles away from the South Wales town, entertaining in the towns and villages of Devon and Cornwall. Cardiff, meanwhile, was in the grip of unparalleled excitement at the opening of the Fine Arts, Industrial and Maritime Exhibition. After years of intense preparation, the official opening and grand procession through the streets of the town had arrived finally.

The stage was set and according to local press reports "nothing had been forgotten or overlooked". The exhibition organisers' plans to promote public awareness of the grand and fantastical displays and pageants would surely surpass every visitor's expectations. To stroll amongst the many and varied exhibits on show across the fifty-acre site would give visitors an experience to remember. There would be sports events each day in which the public could participate, and competitive cycling on the especially constructed wooden cycling track.

No expense had been spared. The elaborate facades and public buildings, designed by Victorian architect Edwin Seward, were testament to the executive committee's commitment to the project. The arts and history of Cardiff jostling for space with displays on the industrial and maritime pursuits of the country.

Local newspapers reported the weather on the morning of Saturday 2nd May "dawned dull and threatening".

Prospects for an improved outlook with a promise of an uncertain climate clearing later in the day. By the afternoon the weather had improved much to the delight of the thousands of local residents and visitors who were arriving in the town centre and taking up the best vantage points throughout the procession route.

The earliest arrivals claimed the best positions to watch the afternoon's proceedings. Prime views opposite the Town Hall in St. Mary Street were completely occupied by midday. The tree-lined road leading to the main entrance of the exhibition in Park Place was proving equally popular.

Those gathered outside the Town Hall would be able to witness the arrival of Lord Windsor, the Exhibition President and Mayor of Cardiff, and the many elaborately robed guests. Everyone hoped the sun would break through the overcast sky in time.

Final arrangements were checked and then checked again before departure of the Grand Procession at 2 o'clock. Sixty horse-drawn carriages with all the attending dignitaries would commence from outside the Town Hall in St. Mary Street.

Lord Windsor hosted a special luncheon for one hundred and sixty invited guests ahead of the Grand Procession. Members of Parliament from the Houses of Commons and Lords, Mayors of South Wales Boroughs, Swansea, Newport,

Tenby, Lampeter, Hereford and Carmarthen, the Mayor of the City of Bristol and the principal commercial men of Cardiff and district, all graced the town with their presence. Lunch would be served in the magnificent Assembly Rooms of the Town Hall. The day was a celebration for the people of the town too.

By early afternoon the weather had brightened as morning clouds gave way to blue skies. One report suggested, "The day was beautifully fine with the vast attendance of the people present who appeared in costumes suitable for May."

At fifteen minutes to one o'clock a line of horse-drawn open carriages and guests were arriving at the steps of the Town Hall to be received by Lord Windsor; resplendent in his Mayorial robes, the weight of responsibility endorsed by his ornate gold chain of office. Thousands of people nearby clamoured to see the proceedings and cheered heartily as each guest arrived.

At one o'clock precisely, luncheon was served in the Assembly Rooms, newly decorated "in shades of pink and green fringed with gold" in preparation for the visit by the Prince of Wales to the town and exhibition in June.

Beautiful tiles of soft grey-green and cream in pleasing design lined the interior walls of the stairway. The balustrade of wrought iron, in perfect harmony, wound its sinuous way up to the top floor. An oriel window of fine stained glass offered a view of the exuberant crowds outside and delighted the guests as they made their way to the magnificence of the Assembly Rooms. The *Western Mail* commented two days later on the superb luncheon the guests had enjoyed, taken beneath glass lustre pendants. "The luncheon was one of the best ever given in the town and the general arrangements were calculated to add to the enjoyment of the guests." What delicacies, gastronomic delights and vintage wines these dignitaries consumed were not recorded.

In the newly built banqueting room of the Exhibition Hall at Cathays Park, luncheon was being enjoyed equally by the executive council and the sixteen sectional exhibition committees. These committees had been formed to monitor specific topics at the exhibition, including agriculture, fine art, photography, scientific instruments, maritime and mining. Amongst the important guests invited to the luncheon was architect Mr Edwin Seward. It was his inventive architectural designs that promoted expectations for a successful exhibition. His fine buildings already graced the town: the majestic Coal Exchange in Mount Stuart Square, and the pleasing architecture of the Free Library and Science Museum that dominated The Hayes and Trinity Street.

Thousands of people had been arriving in the town since the early morning and were now lining every street along the route of the procession to the exhibition entrance in tree-lined Park Place. From the Town Hall to the gates of the exhibition, jostling one another with good-natured revelry for the best view, hardly containing their excitement. Brightly coloured bunting decorated the streets, although it was reported that shopkeepers were keeping their "best decorations" for the visit on 27th June by the Prince and Princess of Wales.

However, fine Venetian styled carnival masks had been

erected in Park Place, the route leading to the exhibition entrance gates.

The Grand Entrance, a spectacular illuminated façade in the Moorish style, was an architectural delight with a decorated arch rising forty feet and flanked at each end by towers measuring 350 feet x 100. Erected on the eastern aspect of the parkland, the entrance would be a prelude to the extraordinary designs inside the exhibition.

Advertisements appeared in local newspapers, "Opening this day Saturday May 2nd 1896", extolled the wealth of exciting exhibits, in which visitors could participate and praised the beauty of Cathays Park; where "exceedingly pretty avenues of green foliage on trees could be seen".

The opening ceremony due to take place that afternoon was restricted to invited guests and season ticket holders.

The general public would have to contain their curiosity until after 3 o'clock once the official Opening Ceremony was completed. It was anticipated that thousands of eager visitors would take the opportunity to attend a "Grand Evening Programme", paying the entrance charge of two shillings and sixpence, (reduced to one shilling after 6 o'clock).

Luncheon was drawing to a close in the opulent Assembly Room, adherence to timing forgotten as the guests began to gather again in the Reception Hall and at the entrance doors of the Town Hall.

The clatter of iron-shod hooves over cobbled stones signalled the imminent arrival of sixty conveyances. These horse-drawn carriages had been marshalled at the rear of the Town Hall, lining the length and breadth of Westgate Street, where the Taff River once flowed. As the luncheon had progressed, quiet discourse between liveried drivers mingled with the jingle of harnesses and the satisfied snorts from the horses' nosebags. (The river had been removed to the west of the Arms Park playing fields in the 1840s, to accommodate Brunel's vision of rail and steam.) These conveyances were finally being summoned, impatient to be on the move after the lengthy period of enforced rest.

A crescendo of cheering rang out as Lord and Lady Windsor settled into their carriage. The Mounted Police escort took up position in front of Lord Windsor's coach, followed by the marching band. The band master raised his baton, turned and with more cheers, the procession moved forward to the strains of stirring military marches.

The route from the Town Hall towards Park Place passed the indoor market, recently restored after its destruction by fire, giving a glimpse of St. John's Church, with a brief view of its fine 15th century tower. As the procession approached Castle Arcade, crowds of people spilled out from its arched entrance. Every window in the High Street a blur of waving arms and flags. They turned into Duke Street with an expert flick of the whip and slap of the reins. The noise of cheering mingled with jingling harness and carriage wheels as they headed towards Queen Street, where the East Gate to the old medieval town once stood. A variety of shops and emporiums now lined either side, and on this day it was empty of trams but filled with hundreds of "well-dressed people" waving Union flags and Welsh flags in equal measure. Despite the procession beginning later than planned the crowd remained in fine spirits. Children perched on fathers' shoulders had the best view, as excitement rippled up Park Place announcing the imminent arrival of the Grand Procession.

Patience was rewarded as a few minutes before 3 o'clock, the carriage with Lord and Lady Windsor entered Park Place, halting in front of the majestic exhibition entrance. They were followed by pairs of trotting horses, each pulling one of the other sixty conveyances.

Sun shone on the braid and buttons of scarlet uniformed Officers, the fur-trimmed robes and Chains of Office of each visiting Mayor and their ladies, and Politicians of both Houses.

The Procession was met at the entrance gates by Mr Robert Forest, Chairman of the executive committee, together with other committee members. Each guest, whilst acknowledging the cheers and applause, was welcomed by Mr Forest before being escorted into the Grand Exhibition Hall. Mayor, Parliamentary notable, Judge, Magistrate, the Judiciary and members of the clergy all passed through the entrance portal and into the expanse of the Reception Hall where they could see for the first time the range of exhibits.

A fine representation of "Old Cardiff", the town as it would have been in the 17th century to the forefront. To the right of "Old Cardiff" was the Fine Art Gallery exhibiting 800 works of art and antiquities. This would prove one of the most popular exhibits with the many visitors over the six months.

The assembled worthies would have time after the opening ceremony to view at leisure the maritime, mining and general exhibits. They glanced right and left as they passed en route to the Rosebery Concert Hall, where the official opening ceremony would take place. This was another example of the splendid buildings designed by Mr Seward and advertised as "having a seating capacity of some 9,000".

The impressive platform would later stage a variety of entertainment; choirs, military bands and orchestras of fine repute who would be performing throughout the six months of the Exhibition, from the beginning of May until its closure in early October.

However, on this day 2nd May 1896, the focus was on the Opening Ceremony. Invited guests waited patiently having taken their seats at least an hour before Lord Windsor, the Mayor and President, Lady Windsor and his guests were due to arrive.

At last the event began. The audience and Special Choir of five hundred sang the National Anthem accompanied by the band of the 9th Queen's Royal Lancers and the Glamorgan Volunteer Artillery Band.

The assembled dignitaries heard a rendition of the Old Hundredth (more popularly known as "All people that on earth do dwell"), sung by the audience. The band and choir performed the Hallelujah Chorus. Welsh Soloist, Thomas Evans, delighted everyone with several songs and Welsh hymns. The crowds gathered outside pressed against the entrance gates, eager to catch any slight sound that might escape from the concert hall. They were rewarded as the voice of Thomas Evans escaped from within, and several hundred Welsh voices rose in unison to accompany Thomas' rendition of the Welsh National Anthem Hen Wlad fy Nhadau (Land of my Fathers). One newspaper reported that "the souls of the

Welsh people found a relief in which they revelled". Arrangements had been made for future programmes to include Welsh Hymns to be sung each night in the Exhibition Hall. Described thus by a local reporter "to remind English visitors of the continued existence of the Nobel Race of Morgan".

The performances were enjoyed thoroughly by all. After which, Lord Windsor in his official black robe, richly adorned with gold lace, addressed the guests and audience, making "a fine speech". Mr Edwin Seward then presented Lord Windsor with a Gold Key, a symbolic representation of the Exhibition Building, and Lord Windsor declared the 1896 Fine Arts, Industrial and Maritime Exhibition open.

The crowds dispersed to view the exhibits and to partake in the beauties of the fifty acres of formal and natural gardens. 10,000 fairy lamps decorated The Imperial Gardens, promising a breath-taking sight when lit at night.

The Opening Ceremony and Procession had attracted 50,000 sightseers to the town, an enthusiastic and encouraging response by the Public. Headlines abounded: "Cathays Park a scene of magnificent animation" and "Miniature World of varied wonders"; "An apocalypse of Science and Art"; "Triumphs of Pyrotechnic Skills". The reconstruction of "Old Cardiff"; models of working coal mines, with a lamp room where several miners and lamp men were on hand to invest their knowledge to those curious enough to enquire. Explanations on the essence of a working "Clanny Safety Lamp" proved popular. The maritime section in the Main Hall displayed models of vessels and clothing. There was a cornucopia of exhibits: Colorado gold mine, collections of mineralogy and mining machinery, a photographic section with studio, an "amateur" product section, and articles made by the blind.

The exciting "Kine-option" showed living photographs by aid of electricity. Would the Panorama depicting the "Battle of Waterloo"excite comment? How would visitors react to the "Flying Lady in a state of trance"; the Haunted Swing; or Borlands' Electric Switchback Railway, 1,000 feet in length; or the working model of a dairy and biscuit factory? Would a reproduction of Shakespeare's house impress, or the beauty of Professor Hemmings' "Original Eve's Crystal Gardens"?

There was so much to enjoy: the exotic Indian Bazaarwith working ants and an African jungle with live animals, lions, monkeys, crocodiles and a giraffe; spectacular watershows of the *Siege of Santiago*, an operatic re-enactment of the 1578 battle (in Chile) between Sir Francis Drake ("El Draque") and Don Pedro de Valdez would be performed each evening on the purpose built lake; an artificial lead-lined canal illuminated by thousands of prismatic gas lamps as darkness descended. Coracles, water cycles and boats for hire, bobbed invitingly on the waters of the lake tempting visitors to test their skills.

At the end of the canal was a strategically placed bandstand where military bands would perform regularly.

Another bandstand sited near the Dutch Cocoa House. Here, Mr Wolff would conduct The Old World Band through a toe-tapping programme of popular music.

When curiosity was satisfied and demands by the footsore required liquid or more substantial refreshment, tearooms, dining rooms, restaurants and bars were on hand to satisfy the needs of the most discerning.

Refreshments could be taken in a choice of restaurants. Luncheon would be served in the first class dining room of the Indian Bazaar from noon until 3pm at two shillings and sixpence. Teas cost one shilling and were served from 3pm until 6pm. Table d'hote dinner cost three shillings and sixpence, available between the hours of 6pm and 9pm.

Other choices were available for visitors throughout the day at the Oriental Bazaar, whose menu offered "Hot and Cold joints with 2 veg (sic), bread and cheese for one shilling and sixpence". And after 3pm a "popular tea at a popular price", all served in fine, light, modern and airy surroundings.

Towards the end of the opening day, a procession of cyclists, ladies and gentlemen, progressed through the town ending at the exhibition.

Appropriately clad men in tweed or plaid knickerbockers and ladies demure in ankle length skirt and crisp white blouse, were all keen to parade upon the newly constructed wooden cycle track. The gathered public expressed their approval with cheers and flag waving. The cycle track would become the launch site for the ascents by balloon of Monsieur Gaudron and from where Mademoiselle Albertina would make her fateful flight.

All thoughts, however, were turned towards the final event of the opening day. Publicity posters boasted, "With a cast of hundreds, the first performance of the Grand water spectacular the operatic *Siege of Santiago*."

Advanced sales of season and day tickets were very

encouraging and the Exhibition Executive agreed the success of the opening day would attract advance sales even further. Advertisements extolling the Fine Arts, Industrial and Maritime Exhibition had proved successful. Thousands of visitors had travelled to Cardiff. They had lined the streets to watch the procession, bought entrance tickets, and spent their money freely in the town and at the exhibition site.

As the evening drew to a close the first of many firework displays lit up the May night sky and the castle in soft silhouette; the ancient ruins and gardens of the Friary also beneficiaries of the illuminations.

The Exhibition President, Committee members and Council Officers relieved as their plans, hopes and anticipated successes had been realised.

Every aspect of their enterprise appeared to have fallen into place. However, they would be called upon very soon to defend their hastily made decisions and to resolve unimaginable outpourings of blame, rumour and accusation.

— CHAPTER ELEVEN —

By the middle of July, the exhibition had settled into the rhythm of the town. Visitor numbers had surpassed projected expectations. A few amendments had been suggested and approved by the executive committee. The concessionaires had also refined their presentations, with the permission of the committee. Admission tickets were reduced to half price on three evenings each week. Public opinion proved emphatically in favour as they embraced the opportunity to visit the exhibition.

The popular water performance, *Siege of Santiago* had been revised with even more spectacular features and attractions than before, as announced in the local papers.

Every week a Grand Athletic Sports event was held in the sports arena. Teams and individuals from across the country competed against one another in track and field competitions. Competitors hoped to win much sought after medals and perhaps to emulate their great sporting heroes who had competed only a few weeks previously in April at "The Games of the 1st Olympiad" in Athens, the first modern Olympics.

The Cycle Track was the venue for daily foot races and

cycle competitions. Comical sports, too, were now a daily feature in the Sports Arena, to which members of the public were invited to participate.

The committee had announced, "A gratifying financial position," stating "two thirds of the proposed Fund appeared to be guaranteed". A total of £18,514 had been taken in the first eleven weeks; a further £10,000 needed to meet outstanding expenses during the remaining eleven weeks.

Figures published in the local press showed concessionaires recouped £6,602 whilst sales of season tickets and entrance fees had produced a further £11,912.

During this period of exuberance, there arrived in Cardiff a performer who would hopefully boost the committee's finances even further. Had visitor numbers shown any sign of declining, the appearance of "Professor" Auguste Eugene Gaudron and his aeronautic displays would surely regenerate enthusiasm.

Gaudron's contract with William Hancock had come to an end on Friday 10th July. He said goodbye to William and Sophie, headed for Torquay Station, and boarded a Great Western train for Cardiff, his wife having travelled from their home in London to join him.

The Gaudrons' arrival in Cardiff occurred sometime during the weekend of 11th and 12th July. Louisa's appearance in Cardiff on Sunday 12th July coincided with that of M. Gaudron. Whether these arrangements had been made whilst they were both in Torquay – to meet up with the Gaudrons at an appointed time and place – has not been established. What is known is that the couple settled into their comfortable centrally situated lodgings at a pleasant house, in Edward Street. Convenient for Cathays Park, the Fine Arts exhibition, the town centre and railway station. Louisa, however, appeared to walk the town in search of lodgings.

His contractual obligations at the exhibition were for a period of one week, the first flight to commence the following day on Monday 13th.

As soon as Alma Beaumont had successfully completed her final flight in Torquay, the bulky paraphernalia of balloons, parachutes and lifebelts had been crated up and despatched to Cardiff, arriving safely in time for "Prof" Gaudron's first planned appearance. Several balloons would be on show, some used as advertising mediums at the exhibition. All the equipment would have to be checked thoroughly. Parachutes, harnesses, trapeze bars, netting, lifebelts, each item carefully unpacked from its crate in readiness for the great man's first flight. He had been contracted by the exhibition concessionaires to make only three appearances on three separate occasions over the next seven days.

Into this heady mix of jubilant anticipation arrived a naïve innocent, the catalyst for this real life Victorian melodrama a breath away from its final denouement. The participants had gathered, a curious public waited. Their appetite for excitement and thrills would become the culpable and the guilty.

Born Louisa Maud Evans, known for most of her brief life as Louie Crinks, and hiding her real identity behind the name Grace Parry. And when fame and fortune seemed to be beckoning, she adopted yet another name the exotic pseudonym of Mademoiselle Albertina. An affectionate reference to Albert her young half-brother perhaps? Was this Louisa Maud, or Louie Crinks, or even Grace Parry's choice of "stage" name? The girl must have been as confused as it was possible for any young woman to be.

Contemporary records revealed a baby who was given away by her mother; a young woman handed over to a travelling circus; and an impressionable girl seduced by glamour and promises of fame, fortune and celebrity. The gullibility of the girl manipulated, and exploited. She would perform for public approbation and other peoples' financial gains. Alone and with no-one to protect her or guide her how could she become anything, achieve anything, when she didn't have an identity?

It was whilst coping with the potential for mental mayhem that she climbed onto the wooden seat of a balloon for the first time, to parachute from thousands of feet above the town of Cardiff. This is not a fantasy; or a fairy tale. What follows is fact, the true account of a young woman coerced into a bizarre act of bravado that remains beyond belief.

The Hancock Family

Hancock's No.1 four-abreast Gallopers, Motorcar Switchback and Helter Skelter at Redruth, with a lineof shows along the left hand side, all with canvas show banners showing the entertainments to be found on the inside of the booths.

Mr and Mrs Crinks with Louisa aged ten.   Mary Ann Evans, the mother.

HMS Adelaide at Devonport on which Andrew Evans' served.

Frontage of the Fine Arts Exhibition 1896.

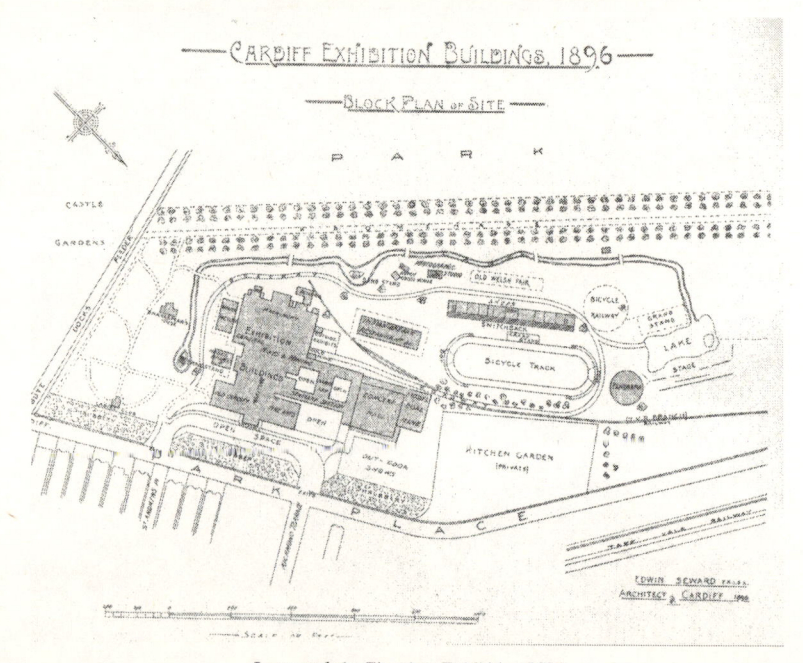

Layout of the Fine Arts Exhibition 1896

"Santiago" stage and lake.

Canals and water cycle.

A sketch of Louisa as Mademoiselle Albertina.

M. Gaudron

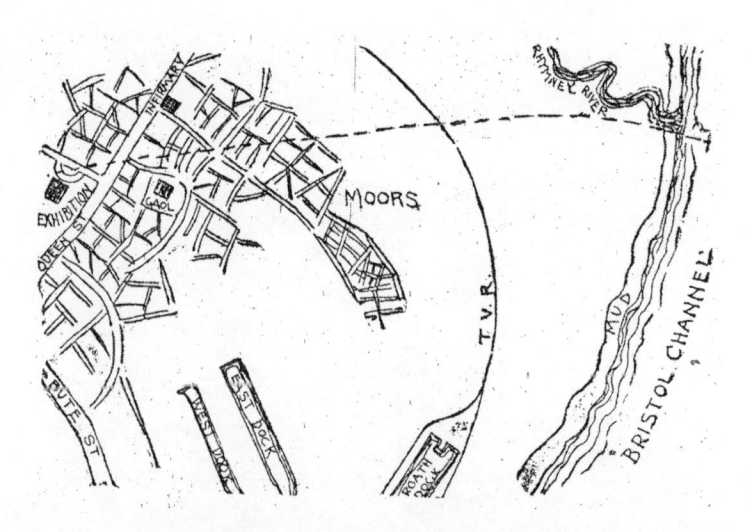

The dotted line shows the course taken by the balloon. The parachutist is said to have dropped where the dotted line ends.

Alma Beaumont   Mary Waggett

Artists impression of where Louisa's body was found.

Beese tea rooms, Conham 2015.

Beese tea rooms, Conham 1890s.

Inlet where Louisa's body was found, 2014.

The belfry of St Mary the Virgin church, Nash 2015.

Waterloo Inn
&
St Mary the Virgin church,
Nash 2015

Mary Ann and Stephen Baker with their ice cream stall, Bristol.

Cardiff Old Town Hall, St Mary Street, 1890s.

Artists impression of Louisa's funeral at Cathays cemetery 1896.

Louisa Maud Evans' grave and tomb stone 1896.

— CHAPTER TWELVE —

On the evening of Sunday 12th July (1896) the Pugh family of number nine Pearson Street, a terraced house close to Cardiff's busy Castle Road, were alerted to a visitor by a knock on the door On their doorstep stood a girl of slight stature, clutching a small brown paper package, blue eyes anxious, long hair tied behind her ears and held in place by a coloured bow. Beside her stood a landlady from Shakespeare Street. The two women exchanged pleasantries before the girl made her hurried introduction. "My name is Grace Parry. I am the sister of M. Gaudron the famous aeronaut." She continued with undue haste explaining that she was in need of a room for the night. Despite Mrs Pugh's reluctance the girl was admitted; the lateness of the Sunday evening a consideration for the landlady's kindly gesture. The door of number nine closed behind her. Louisa had found a bed for that night at least. It had been an eventful day.

Twenty-four hours had passed since she left Torquay, the Hancocks, her guardians and employers and her new found friends, Henrietta and Harriet. The train journey to Cardiff had been exciting, although perhaps longer than she had imagined. Her arrival at the Great Western Railway

Station in Cardiff was much later than she anticipated. Had she travelled on her own? Was this her first visit to the Welsh town? If so, this would explain Louisa's search for lodgings so late at night. If, however, she had been accompanied on her journey, her travelling companion may have recommended suitable theatrical lodgings but preferred not to be part of the procedure.

Although her earlier visit to Shakespeare Street proved fruitless, at least the landlady had offered to take her to the Pugh's house in Pearson Street, where she planned to lodge for several days. Unfortunately it wasn't to be. Louisa's luck was diminishing by the hour.

She awoke the following morning, Monday 13th, determined to find Gaudron. Having followed the Frenchman to the Welsh town her priority was to locate him as soon as possible. She knew he was contracted to perform at the Fine Arts exhibition that week, and that was where she hoped to find him. They did meet later that afternoon in the pleasure gardens of Cathays Park. Why had he told Louisa about his engagement in Cardiff? Was he surprised to see her? Or had they arranged this meeting whilst in Devon? And was he planning to involve the girl in future ballooning events?

Whatever his motives and involvement with her arrival in Cardiff, when questioned by the press and public several days later, he failed to give a satisfactory answer. He would continue to change his story, believing his celebrity status protected him from censure.

When returning to her lodgings later that evening, she was confronted by the landlady. She must vacate her room as "visitors were arriving". Mrs Pugh had become suspicious of Louisa's lack of luggage, shortage of money and her constant boasting about being a "professional" and the sister of M. Gaudron, the famous aeronaut. Two evenings later, Wednesday 15th, she gathered up her meagre possessions and walked away from number 9 Pearson Street.

Without any idea where to find lodgings, she sought out her only contact in the bustling industrial town. It was after midnight when she knocked the door of number 19 Edward Street, the temporary residence of Monsieur and Madame Gaudron.

Despite the late hour, the knock at the door was answered by landlady Mrs Warsow. What must she have thought about the arrival of this young woman who appeared at midnight seeking the Gaudrons?

The explanations for this extraordinary occurrence must have been accepted as a bed was hastily made up for Louisa on the sofa. What was Madame Gaudron's response? Did a slight unease of mind afflict Auguste Gaudron?

However, whatever the Gaudrons thought that night, on the following morning, much to the delight of Louisa, accommodation was found in a lodging house on the opposite side of the road with a Mrs Watson at 26 Edward Street. It was agreed between all interested parties that whilst Louisa would sleep at number 26, her meals would be taken with Monsieur and Madame Gaudron at number 19. She was near enough for them to maintain a collective and benevolent eye, though at a suitable distance from the young woman should there be any suggestion of impropriety. Louisa must have considered herself very fortunate to receive the attention of such internationally famous personages. The lifestyle she craved during her travels through Cornwall and Devon was a heartbeat away.

Louisa told him of her ambition to become a balloonist whilst they were in Torquay. She travelled to Cardiff, believing he would train her as an aeronaut, and if she picked up the rudiments of ballooning quickly, would perform with him at his next engagement in Scotland.

There was a determination akin to foolhardiness about this young woman's desire to take to the skies. She had been captivated by the aura of celebrity, fuelled by observing the adulation showered on Alma Beaumont and Auguste Gaudron, the two stars of the Cornish skies. She had become excited by the prospect of finding fame and fortune.

Realisation began to dawn at the freedom she had found after running away from her guardians and the funfair. A freedom to make decisions. Now she could follow paths previously unobtainable. The possibilities were infinite; she had choice at last; she was no longer an extension of other people's whims or wishes. There would be no more domestic chores for "Aunt" Sophie Hancock. Or working at Todd's Cloth Factory near her home in Bristol, or travelling around the West Country with the Crinks, her adoptive parents. Her first act of independence had been accomplished when she had boarded the train at Torquay railway station in Devon.

Whilst the train rattled its way toward Cardiff, she had planned her new life. From this moment on she was to do as she pleased.

To become an Aeronaut, sailing up into the sky, parachuting back to earth to the sounds of the cheering crowds below. A promise of fine financial rewards too. Hadn't Monsieur Gaudron suggested he might pay her five pounds for each flight? Here lay her future; people would speak of her, applaud her; her exploits recounted in newspapers; her name on advertising posters in the manner of Alma Beaumont.

Whilst an exciting future awaited Louisa Maud Evans, and her desire to find fame and celebrity would be realised beyond her wildest imaginings, this was a naïve innocent girl ripe for manipulation and exploitation.

She had settled in after the first uncertain days following her arrival, absorbing the atmosphere of the town as it flourished through the popularity of the Fine Arts Exhibition. And Louisa was entranced.

Soon after her arrival in Cardiff she became acquainted with John Owen, a young man of similar age, a participant in the epic open-air water pageant, *The Siege of Santiago*. The daily performances of this extravaganza were just one of the many popular events at the exhibition. The pageant included a cast of several hundred performers, of actors, singers, an orchestra and a choir.

John and Louisa soon became close friends and confidantes. She became acquainted with many of the performers at the exhibition, who took the young woman to their hearts.

Members of The Old World Band, whose music could be

heard every day throughout the grounds of the parkland; the families of Royal Epping Forest Gypsies, whose brightly coloured tents could be seen alongside the cycle track; famous knife thrower, Monsieur Vallette, a popular performer at the exhibition, became something of a confidant too. They all befriended this young woman, perhaps recognising her need for acceptance and friendship.

Louisa, usually a quiet, diffident girl blossomed in this environment. The funfairs, stalls, bazaars were not entirely unknown to her; mirroring her experiences of the past few months of travel with the Hancock family.

The days that followed passed in a blur of activity for Louisa and the Gaudrons. Auguste Gaudron prepared for his performances due to take place from the spacious cycle track, when two more performances were scheduled. One flight was planned during the Temperance Fete on Wednesday 15th of July, and his last ascent was due to take place on the evening of Saturday 18th.

Louisa meanwhile was familiarising herself with the historic town, her daily walk to the exhibition grounds took her along the route of the busy canal where coal barges, heavy with "black gold" plied back and forth, from valley pits to the busy Bute docks. Her journey led her towards Queen Street where a complement of shops displayed the latest designs in furniture and furnishings. Ironmongers, milliners and drapers, fishmongers and florists, solicitors, jewellers, patent offices and surgeons were in neighbourly competition with tea merchants, pork purveyors, dentists and photographic studios, each jostling for custom. In the centre of these gastronomic and fashionable delights was one of the town's favourite entertainment venue, the popular Empire Palace of Varieties. Those who sought a more dramatic evening's entertainment could treat themselves to Marcos J. Hydes Number One Company's performance of the modern Irish play *Famine* at the Theatre Royal just a short walk away in St. Mary's Street.

To reach the Fine Arts Exhibition safely, expediency and careful negotiation of Queen Street was a skilful necessity. The profusion of tramlines embedded in the cobbles tripped up the unwary or too hasty. Eastbound and westbound horsedrawn tramcars, a vibrant livery of green or yellow, rattled along the routes to "Roath via Newport Road" or "Canton via Cardiff Bridge", and demanded one penny from every traveller bound for town or docks.

Louisa's exploration of the town would have taken her past the walls of the castle, where the 3rd Marquess was in residence with his wife and young family having expressed a wish to visit the Fine Arts Exhibition. His patronage welcomed by the organisers and the populace of the town.

The design by the brilliant and oft-times controversial Victorian architect William Burges had transformed the Bute family's medieval house into an iconic statement of Neo-Gothic Victorian fantasy so beloved by these two 19th Century Romantics.

Although Louisa would not have seen inside the extensive castle grounds, she could not have ignored the majestic 1870s gold-figured clock tower, or the grey-brown crenellated outer walls that dominated the town on the approaches from the Welsh Valleys and lands to the north of the town.

*

At Cathays Park, Auguste Gaudron's plans for the week were in need of some unexpected reorganisation. After a successful flight on the evening of Monday 13th July, and although feted enthusiastically on his return, the balloon had been damaged on landing. With the Grand Temperance event due two days later on Wednesday 15th, he deployed the replacement balloon, only to discover this envelope had developed a leak and failed to inflate properly. He was unable to perform much to the disappointment of the many thousands who had arrived to celebrate the Grand Temperance event.

The Press report of the incident stated, "The plucky Frenchman was much distressed and felt the disappointment as keenly as the crowd. All was in readiness, the pull of the balloon slight. M. Gaudron climbing onto the looped seat found the balloon could not raise him high enough to clear a large tree."

As Gaudron alighted from the loop of the balloon, despite sufficient gas being retained to launch it, the balloon was buoyant enough to be torn from its restraints. The helpers who were holding it in position lost their collective grips and watched in dismay as the balloon sailed away and headed towards the centre of the town, causing a great commotion amongst the public when the half-inflated envelope landed in the busy shopping area of Queen Street.

No person was injured and no property damaged, although the tills of Jesse Williams the Chemist at No.95 may have benefited from an increased demand for restorative smelling salts.

— CHAPTER THIRTEEN —

By Monday 20th the damaged balloon had been repaired. He had been retained for a further week, and so Gaudron's evening performance would take place as advertised. Decorative fairy lights in abundance illuminated the vast wooden cycle and athletic tracks from where the launch would take place. The hundreds of spectators gathered round the track and filling the seats of the Grand Stand expressed their enthusiasm as the dapper little man appeared amongst them.

The restaurant was situated nearby in the Indian Bazaar, and according to the advertisements, "displayed the style of the exotic"; it was full of visitors enjoying the fine dining. Diners could also watch the launch of the balloon from their tables.

Once Gaudron had climbed aboard the sphere of the balloon and taken his place on the narrow seat slung beneath the gas-filled apparatus, the balloon, freed from restraining ropes, hovered briefly then began to rise above the vast exhibition grounds, as laughter and music from the carousels and gallopers at Studts Old Welsh fair accompanied him into the evening sky.

As Gaudron floated away, quickly reaching several thousand feet over the bunting-bedecked town, the noise and bustle of the restaurant and the chatter of its patrons ceased. Attention directed away from gossip and gastronomy to the spectacular launch of the balloon.

Despite the lack of directional equipment on board he avoided the hazards of industrial and maritime obstacles to the south and east of the town. Enthusiastic applause followed him from the thousands of visitors at the exhibition. Many thousands more watched from across Cardiff and the surrounding countryside. The best vantage points had been settled upon earlier by local families, who arrived with bulging picnic baskets intent on watching the evening's spectacle in comfort. A popular viewing place was the promontory known as Penarth Head, a few miles to the south west of the town.

As the balloon reached a height of 9,000 feet or so, Gaudron leapt from the suspended seat. His weight easily snapped the length of thin cord that attached the parachute to the balloon's outer netting.

One press report caught the essence of the moment: "He makes his parachute descent from the clouds. To get this elevation he has to go up in a balloon and the fun of watching the preliminary performance and exciting start of the voyageur is worth every half penny at the turn styles."

On this Monday evening he descended without incident, thankful not to repeat the drama of the previous Saturday evening's performance, initially agreed with the concessionaires, to have been his last in Cardiff. During his descent on that particular evening, his return to earth had not been in accordance with his pre-flight plan. As M. Gaudron floated beneath the open canopy he realised he was heading towards the ruddy glow of several activefurnace chimneys of the Dowlais Steel Works, east of the town centre.

These chimneys were very close to the busy Bute docks and Taff Vale Docks Railway. He managed to avoid landing on top of the furnace chimneys, or suffering an even worse fate of falling into one of them.

As the parachute floated slowly down he clung to the wooden bar without benefit of a safety harness, his usual mode d'employ. He dangled beneath the canopy as it drifted over the top of these fiery obstacles, when another hazard presented itself. To the west of the chimneys lay the Bute East docks, an expanse of enclosed water. Here ships from across the world were moored alongside wharves awaiting the loading of Welsh coal. These chunks of "black gold", hewn from the many pits in the mining valleys of South Wales, filled the hundreds of open topped coal trucks close-packed nearby.

These sailing vessels were about to share their watery basin with a parachuting Frenchman. Gaudron splashed into the water with a force that startled the resting seabirds.

Fortunately he had taken the precaution of wearing a lifebelt which saved him from total immersion. Despite the parachute sinking below the surface his head and shoulders remained above the waterline.

His rescue from the watery dock basin was achieved efficiently and in no time he had returned to the exhibition ground where he was given a hero's welcome. The horse drawn vehicle surrounded on all sides by cheering crowds.

Each ascent and descent could place aeronauts in uncontrolled danger, as the performances on the evenings of 13th and 18th July had proved.

The popularity of these balloon and parachute events was extraordinary. The public clamoured for more performances. A captive balloon (held by retaining ropes) was on show in the grounds of the exhibition, an advertisement for future launches causing heightened anticipation amongst the visitors.

So much public interest was shown in these performances that the committee and concessionaires realised the potential for extra flights. A substantial financial boost to the profits had already been generated. The first week of Gaudron's performances resulted in an increased attendance at the exhibition of over 57,000 visitors.

The concessionaires responsible for the shops, tea rooms and dining rooms were also experiencing increased profits. The exhibition was due to close at the beginning of October, and by mid-July had reached the half way mark of its six month run. Additional revenue at that time would be beneficial to everyone.

Ticket sales were again boosted when the Temperance Fete came to town.

It seemed as though the world and his wife descended on Cardiff during Wednesday 15th July, the Fete's gala day.

The occasion of the Great Temperance Fete organised by the Cardiff and District Band of Hope Union encouraged the public to visit the town in their thousands. They "wedged themselves into buildings, swarmed over the grounds" and eclipsed all previous attendance figures. The streets were crowded with "excursionists" as described by one local news reporter.

An initiative by Railway and Steamboat Companies offered greatly reduced fares, eagerly taken advantage of by the delighted populous.

Admission charges to the Fete and Fine Arts Fair were reduced, sixpence for adults and threepence for children, with one third of the takings to be donated to the Band of Hope Union and two thirds to the Promoters of the exhibition.

Each of the Temperance Societies in South Wales was represented. 10,000 of their members gathered in Westgate Street to participate in the afternoon procession, with brass, drum and fife bands enlivening the "processionists" en route to the exhibition entrance gates.

Once inside the entrance gates, the eagerness with which parties of children made "a mighty rush" for the merry-go-round and switchback rides of Studts Old Welsh Fair was matched by their parents' enjoyment of the exhibits, the sports and comic sports events, all over-subscribed.

The captive balloon attracted considerable attention. Unfortunately, there would be no balloon flight by M. Gaudron that evening, due, as explained previously, to the damage caused to the balloon two evenings before.

The disappointed crowds dispersed en masse from around the cycle track, causing a lottery for seats in the grandstand overlooking the lake, the ideal spot from which to view the spectacle of *The Siege of Santiago*.

Despite a degree of grumbling by non-temperance visitors who were without recourse to whisky and beer due to Mr Culley's "stop-tap" regime, it was reported that "a rattling good business was done in ginger beer, lemonade and lime juice".

The review by the organising committee and concessionaires at the end of the day declared it was a most memorable occasion, and a resounding success. Such positive factors needed to be exploited. They approached M. Gaudron with two requests which came as no great surprise to the Frenchman. He was asked to make additional flights, requested firstly by Mr Cundall (General_Exhibition Superintendent) and secondly by Mr Culley (a member of the Exhibition Committee). Would M. Gaudron agree to being retained for a further week, to continue with his daring aerial displays? And could he introduce a lady balloonist and parachutist to the programme? The public's appetite for these aeronautical displays demanded the inclusion of such a thrilling spectacle.

The first indication that M. Gaudron was planning to satisfy their request for a lady aeronaut was the appearance of a small paragraph in a local paper. Headed "Another Balloon Ascent", it continued with the following information: "To-night (Saturday) M. Gaudron is announced to make another ascent in a balloon and descent by the parachute. The first balloon used on Monday has been repaired and everything bids fair for a successful journey.

"That an enormous concourse of people will watch the adventurer goes without saying. M. Gaudron has been engaged for three more ascents next week. He is to go up on Monday, Wednesday and Friday and for alternate days the concessionaires have secured Miss Alma Beaumont, an aeronaut of great daring and increasing reputation. Thus there will be one of these popular balloon ascents every night."

It was printed in the *Western Mail* on Saturday 18th July, six days after Louisa had arrived in Cardiff. Where had the press acquired this information, and from whom? Whilst it cannot be verified exactly who the source was, Monsieur and Madame Gaudron both knew about Alma Beaumont and her forthcoming marriage. M. Gaudron knew beyond any doubt that she was unavailable. Two weeks previously on 10th July, Alma had travelled to London with her intended future husband Herbert Conway.

Their contract with the Hancocks in Torquay was at an end. Miss Beaumont had resigned, severing her involvement with Gaudron's company and, at that time, any future engagements as a professional aeronaut. Auguste had asked her to reconsider but his plea was rejected.

A contract signed several weeks previously by Gaudron with the Glasgow authorities in Scotland confirmed he and a lady parachutist would appear there at the end of July. His reputation was under serious threat should he fail to honour the contract. His famous lady parachutist had resigned. She was giving up the profession in order to be married.

Compounded by suggestions of a rift between them, as her future husband had cited financial differences between his fiancée and Gaudron, another reason for her decision to leave. Herbert Conway delighted in announcing there had been heated discussions concerning money matters between the two men on several occasions.

So there can have been no doubt in the Frenchman's mind that Alma would not be appearing with him in Scotland and definitely not at the Fine Arts Exhibition in Cardiff. The pressure on him from the exhibition committee and concessionaires to engage a lady aeronaut and his eagerness to oblige had placed him in a difficult situation. Both parties were conscious of the extra revenue the appearance of an exotically named and flamboyantly dressed lady balloonist would generate. Perhaps he thought Alma would change her mind and agree to appear at one more event? She did not. Auguste Gaudron allowed the promise of extra financial rewards to cloud his judgement. How was he to maintain his credibility and resolve this request by the Exhibition Committee satisfactorily?

— CHAPTER FOURTEEN —

John Owen was determined to disguise his concern for his companion. There had been a marked change in his friend over the past two days. Preoccupied and subdued beneath an air of despondency, nothing had lightened her mood despite the prospect of visiting their favourite exhibits.

Where previously she was happy and excited by every aspect of the exhibition, now she was nervous and anxious not to be seen in public. Despite his gentle teasing, she had revealed nothing of significance except her silence. His assumption was that it was connected in some way with the flamboyant French balloonist.

Since becoming acquainted with her six days previously, although he thought it may have been seven, they had become good friends. She had revealed little of herself or her past. He had gleaned eventually her previous involvement with a travelling fair and circus, and that she had recently journeyed from Torquay in Devon to meet with friends in Cardiff one of whom, the French Aeronaut, was contracted to perform this very week at the Fine Arts exhibition.

He expressed surprise when first she told him about her involvement with the aeronautics, and felt he should make known his fears for her safety. Her laughter had eased his concern. She had spoken of previous experiences, surely indicating insurance against any unlikely mishap.

John considered whether she was a little in love with the French aeronaut. She became so animated when talking about him. If so, was this now the cause of her nervousness and insistence to avoid being seen in public? Whatever her concerns, she was determined to keep them secret.

Each afternoon they had enjoyed exploring the Exhibition Grounds together, visiting the exotic, the amusing and the fantastical. Befriended by the Epping Forest gypsies the young couple had been welcomed into their homely caravans and the brightly coloured tents that nudged the perimeter of the elevated cycle track, where thousands of spectators enjoyed the variety of sporting and cycling competitions. John reflected on how they spent fun filled days peddling water cycles along the bends and twists of the lead-lined canal, waving acknowledgement as they passed "The Old World Band" whose popular music floated out from the island bandstand.

They found pleasure in listening to the music of the Military Bands together, and pleasure in each other's company. On one occasion she had expressed a wish to visit *The Siege of Santiago*, the water spectacular in which

John performed. To his delight his pretty friend had arrived that evening, watching the performance from her seat in the grandstand surrounded by an audience equally enthralled.

Afterwards they walked through the maze of stalls and mechanical rides of Studts Old Welsh Fair, strolling beneath the wonder of modern electrical illuminations that lit up the tree-lined pathway of the Promenade "affording pleasant walks under shades of lofty elms". She had enjoyed the historical water spectacular very much, her enthusiasm genuine. But today (Monday 20th July), all was not as it had seemed. Something or someone had upset his dear friend. There was no way of changing her mood, so they agreed to part and arranged to meet again later that evening.

Gaudron meanwhile was deliberating on his friendship with this young woman and wondering whether he had been too hasty in encouraging her interest in aeronautics.

Her arrival in Cardiff and determination to learn the art of ballooning had at first seemed to be opportune. It offered this canny businessman a resolution to the problem of fulfilling his contractual arrangements in Glasgow. He agreed to instruct her in the skills she would need as a professional aeronaut. If all went according to Gaudron's plans and Louisa's dreams, the training would begin at the earliest opportunity. There would be time after completion of his performances in Cardiff. The final launch was due on Saturday 18th July. Arrangements were in hand for her to travel to Scotland with him for her first appearance, scheduled for the end of July. These plans, however, unexpectedly changed when Mr Cundall and George Webster, on behalf of the concessionaires, approached Gaudron, with a degree of impatience, seeking an answer to their earlier request regarding the hiring of a lady aeronaut. Despite some misgivings, Gaudron finally confirmed that a lady balloonist would indeed be hired, and would make several ascents and descents the following week. He also agreed to launch on three more evenings, commencing Monday 20th, whilst the lady aeronaut would appear on alternate nights. Her first flight would be the evening of Tuesday 21st.

The clamour by the public for extra flights was satisfied, the pressure to hire a lady aeronaut fulfilled. And now the local newsmen wanted a statement from this brave lady. Louisa felt uncertain and frightened. Frightened that should another newspaper reporter find her, he would ask questions she couldn't answer truthfully.

The press had searched the fifty acres of the exhibition grounds in determined pursuit of this young woman, an assault by the Victorian news hounds to interview this exotic creature and discover the truth about the first lady balloonist to perform at this high-profile event.

An interview with Mademoiselle Albertina would surely reveal fascinating insights into her profession and her lifestyle; a coup for the reporter, publicity for the exhibition and titillation for the curious and sensation-hungry public. She was determined to avoid them, ill equipped and ill prepared for such questioning.

She had been tracked down and interviewed earlier that day by several members of the press, at which time she nervously stated that this would not be her first flight and that she had flown with Professor Gaudron in a captive balloon in Dublin. When questioned further, she confirmed having made several ascents in Cornwall. Louisa decided she must keep away from the exhibition if nothing else was to be revealed.

Where was the French Professor Gaudron? Was he in hiding from overly enthusiastic press interest, avoiding making any statement about Mademoiselle Albertina?

M. Gaudron was also becoming concerned about Louisa (or Grace, as he believed her to be named). He had permitted the offer of tantalising financial rewards from the concessionaires to overrule caution and his better judgement. If she was hiding from reporters, as seemed the case, and displaying signs of nervousness, this would be cause enough to regret the decision to train her.

None of this deception would have been necessary had Alma Beaumont continued to work with him a while longer and agreed to appear in Scotland at the end of July. Had her fiancé, Herbert Conway not interfered, Gaudron believed the present situation would not have arisen. Alma would have agreed to appear in Scotland and could possibly have taken on the role of Lady Aeronaut in Cardiff too. He would not be preparing a novice, an unknown, in the intricacies and potential hazards of taking to the skies in a balloon, or the more dangerous feat of parachuting back to earth unscathed. He admitted reluctantly, the town of Cardiff had proved very difficult to negotiate even for him, an experienced aeronaut with many hundreds of flights and jumps safely executed. .....Launching the balloon from the exhibition grounds had not proved a problem. It was at 6,000 or 7,000 feet, a safe height from which to jump, that the difficulties had arisen. The town spread out beneath the spinning parachutist formed a blurred vision of narrow streets and substantial municipal buildings. Without specific controls attached to the parachute, the direction was determined by experience and the forces of nature. Of course, wind speed and direction were checked prior to a flight and taken into consideration, in order to govern direction and speed of descent. These directional forces gave only an approximation as to where the parachutist would land.

To the south of the town lay the wide, muddy reaches of the Bristol Channel beside which lay the extensive Bute Docks, Dowlais Steel Works and Tharsis Copper works. If the furnace chimneys of the steel works didn't raise alarm in the descending aeronaut, the flames of red and orange lighting up the evening sky, and the dark waters of the East and West Bute docks certainly would. Should an unexpected gust of wind catch under the canopy as it flew high over the open scrub lands of the East Moors, the unfortunate 'chutist would sail beyond land, out of control over the mudflats and the fast flowing waters of the Bristol channel. He comforted himself with the knowledge that the young woman had shown a mature understanding. She listened to his instructions about direction and potential hazards, and studied the map of the town with diligence.

As long as she jumped as instructed, when directly over the Infirmary to the east of the town centre, all would be well. Gaudron may have considered these instructions were simple enough to follow. But what of Louisa and her thoughts on the approaching flight? Were her dreams of fame being realised? It had seemed so exciting when first planning to escape the dull routine of her daily chores and domestic duties. Flattered by the attentions of the French balloonist and Zalva the American high wire artiste, both of whom suggested there could be opportunities for her to train as a circus performer. But now, as the reality of these decisions began to close in on her, she wanted to confide her misgivings to John, although M. Gaudron's insistence impressed upon her to tell no one had to be respected. She wanted so much to tell John of her concerns, of the bothersome reporters trying to find her and also to reveal to him her exciting secret. There was no pleasure to be had in any of this deception. Perhaps she could explain it to him after returning from the balloon flight tomorrow evening.

She would tell him how, whilst touring with the Hancocks, she had watched every flight by Monsieur Gaudron and Miss Beaumont; how she had approached Gaudron seeking an introduction in the art of ballooning, exhibiting a boldness of spirit that had surprised her. John would surely then approve her performances in Cardiff. They were not due to a sudden whim. Gaudron had encouraged her involvement. And hadn't Zalva expressed interest in her joining his troupe?

However, the promise of glamour and financial rewards as an aeronaut had proved a superior choice. She was sure John would understand the need for her deception once explained.

The final days prior to her launch in that flimsy gas-filled receptacle were running out of control. She tried to comprehend the complexity of the instructions from M. Gaudron: a jumble of confusing information about height, wind direction and speed, when and where to jump and the necessity to memorise the plan of the town. If this was not enough to undermine her confidence and enthusiasm, the instructions on how and when to release the steel safety clasps certainly were.

Freeing herself from the sling hanging beneath the balloon when at the point of greatest safety was evidently critical. M. Gaudron had impressed on her she must release when over the Infirmary, the building east of Queen Street, which he assured her she would have no difficulty in recognising.

She would, in all probability, then land in the open space of the East Moor. However, should there be any encounter with water, he emphasised there would be no need for concern as she would be wearing a regulation life belt. On that point he was adamant.

She was being plagued now by reporters from local newspapers, who were demanding interviews with her. The only respite she had was time she spent away from the exhibition grounds with her trusted friend John. She felt a little guilty at the game of deception she was playing. A promise she gave to Gaudron not to reveal anything was almost ignored when earlier in the day the kindly woman dresser, who had assisted with fitting the elaborate costume Louisa would wear, remarked on the pristine condition of the outfit. She told Louisa how she admired her bravery and wouldn't consider such an occupation herself, before then wishing her a safe flight. Such comments threatened Louisa's resolve but she remained silent.

— CHAPTER FIFTEEN —

Her first ascent at the Fine Arts exhibition in Cardiff would take place on the evening of Tuesday 21st. Front-page advertisements in local newspapers stated that, "on Wednesday and Saturday at 7.30pm Prof. A.E. Gaudron in his Daring Parachute Descent and Mdlle Albertino (sic) the celebrated Lady Parachutist on Tuesday, Thursday and Friday at 7.30pm" This was confirmation of her appearance. There would be no turning back.

Earlier on the Tuesday evening Gaudron had insisted she check the equipment. Whether she understood the significance of this and whether she could identify if equipment was safe can only be guessed at.

News reports indicated, "Prior to the ascent there had been a considerable period of uncertain weather, the sky had been overcast with clouds and a brisk downpour of rain threatened." However, by the time she was due to ascend a more optimistic outlook was hinted at: "A smart breeze sprang up from the west and scattered the clouds so effectively that a clear atmosphere succeeded it."

At the appointed time the dresser helped her into a blue cotton sailor-styled blouse with gold trimmings and voluminous knickerbockers; her long blond hair fell in soft curls from under peaked sailor cap. Smart black patent leather ankle boots completed the image. Louisa was transformed.

Mademoiselle Albertina now ready to take centre stage. The cotton blouse was cool against her skin; generous knickerbockers an unimagined freedom from clinging petticoats and draped skirt.

One final item needed to be strapped around her small frame: the cork life belt whose bulky pressure creased the newness of the blue fabric blouse. Mademoiselle Albertina, at last an image of sartorial aeronautic splendour, was excited and nervous in equal measure.

An impression of the young woman was noted by the press, "Mademoiselle Albertina dressed in a sailor costume and knickerbockers, looking very young and diminutive made her appearance on the track at about a quarter to eight."

Walking through the crowds, spontaneous applause surrounded her as she made her way to the platform. Her girlish appearance, her unsophisticated bow and demeanour, in acknowledgement, caused surprised comments from onlookers. One remarked, "Her refined features and girlish blue eyes did not immediately suggest a daring adventurer."

"She was cheered heartily as she took her seat and grasped the hoop of the parachute". The suspended wooden seat swayed beneath the captive balloon as Gaudron attached the safety clips, securing her to the parachute's trapeze bar. He stepped back. Retaining ropes on the balloon were unclipped, handlers released their holds. After a brief moment of silence, the balloon lifted and she sailed upwards catching a last sight of John, a familiar face trapped within the crowded arena. She called to him "Don't forget the milk, tra la la" but her voice was drowned out by the swish of the canopy as it gained height. His reply was lost amongst the cheers. He watched anxiously as the wind carried her rapidly to several thousand feet within a few seconds.

The excitement of a balloon ascent and parachute descent by a lady, a Mademoiselle Albertina, spread to the Roath district and surrounding areas. When questioned later an onlooker recalled "the balloon speedily rose and the fresh breeze blowing at the time, took her clear off the ground in a very short space of time. When the balloon was over Splott (to the east of the town), it seemed to get out of the wind and gradually rose higher and higher. About 12,000 feet had been reached before the girl, a tiny dark speck beneath them aerial globule, let go."

The expectant thousands in the streets of Splott consequently had a splendid view of Mademoiselle as the balloon carried her swiftly, high above the chimney pots.

Another onlooker in the audience at the arena commented that, "the balloon sped upward and upward, until it became very small indeed and the adventuresome lady hanging in the dangling ropes until a mere speck, like a dot at the base of an exclamation… Down and down she fell, until doubts were beginning to be felt as to whether the parachute ever would open. It opened at last, however, and the crowd at the track gave vent to their feelings in a hearty cheer."

Did Louisa hear the cheers from her dizzy height? Did she thrill to the crowds who were enthralled with her? Or was she in a frightened stupor?

The onlooker continued to recount, "everyone commented on why she didn't leave the balloon sooner.

Finally she detached from the balloon, the parachute opening almost simultaneously," (although this contradicts reports by those who said it was very late opening). "She appeared to be stationary for a short period and then she commenced to descend, very slowly. The wind carried her over East Moor and then gradually we lost sight of her as she was blocked by houses."

Those who had been following the passage of the balloon then began to question "whether the fair parachutist would not drop into the sea."

Gaudron who was watching anxiously from the cycle track began to fear that his final instructions were not being adhered to. Whilst he allowed a relieved escape of breath, he was concerned that she had not jumped over the Infirmary as he had told her repeatedly so to do. He realised she had left her descent too late and was now drifting in a south easterly direction toward the Bristol Channel. He had spread a plan of the locality before her, on several occasions, making a point of explaining carefully the buildings she would pass over when in the air. Having estimated as near as possible, direction and speed of the wind, he told her the route the balloon would take and how long it would be, approximately, before she was over the area where she should jump. He emphasised she must anticipate the buildings and should look for and in particular the Infirmary.

Even if she missed this and the wind took her out to sea, he reassured her once again that the life belt would indeed support her. So why, he worried, hadn't she jumped where he'd said.

"I told her to drop over the Infirmary" he would repeatedly say in mitigation. "She'd gone too far south-east, I told her to drop over the Infirmary."

Spectators were also of the opinion that she did not act on M. Gaudron's suggestion, "as the sphere sailed over the East Moor and was above the channel when she came down." Several ventured that had she left the ropes of the balloon when above the Infirmary she would have probably descended on the East Moor. It was hoped that a contingency of boats would be on hand in the channel.

John's single thought was to escape from the crowds pulsing against him. To do as she had bid. Locate a cab and buy some milk. He would follow the direction of the balloon and be there to meet her wherever she landed. He must keep his promise given last evening. An evening he would not forget.

They had met as arranged on the Monday evening, when her state of mind seemed even more troubled.

He would recount to a reporter several days later, "She appeared once or twice to be trembling." His immediate response to her unhappy state: "If she was troubled about the ascent she ought not to go up." Her reply, so the young man continued, was that, "She would go, that she didn't mind." He recalled telling her, "If you are like this tomorrow night I'll burst the balloon so you can't go." She laughed and said she was alright and certainly should go up.

Recalling that previous evening's conversation did not encourage confidence. Where was his friend going to land?

Perhaps the Frenchman would have a better idea. John decided his best option would be to find Gaudron and stay close to him.

As she ascended, the excitement from those who surrounded the cycle track overflowed into the streets nearby. Cheers and applause rippled through the town as Mademoiselle Albertina rose higher and higher becoming visible to the thousands watching her progress. Until she became a dark speck against the faded blue of the evening sky.

When the balloon reached Splott it seemed to get out of the wind and gradually rose even further. Reports of the height inclined towards "12,000 feet being reached before the girl let go," attaining a much greater altitude than that by M. Gaudron. So great had been the interest taken in previous aerial performances by Gaudron, and in particular his undignified ducking in the Bute East Dock a few days previously, it was assumed contingency plans were in hand should the lady parachutist drop in to the sea. Although confidence was also placed in the Board of Trade Life belt she had strapped firmly around her waist, M. Gaudron having been vigorous in his reassurances to Albertina and everyone involved with her launch. The crowds at the exhibition lost sight of her as the parachute descended over the East Moor. Despite the late hour, with dusk closing in, they determined to stay and greet the young adventurer when she returned in triumph. The same excitement was evident with the crowds watching in the Roath district and the Docks surrounds.

Several onlookers observed that the weather could have accounted for the problem Mademoiselle experienced. The overcast sky, a brisk downpour of rain and a high wind threatening did not make for ideal flying conditions.

Those in attendance near the mouth of the Rumney River and many watching from the Docks and Taff Vale Railway were perhaps the first people to realise Albertina was going to land in the sea. The crowds were not concerned as all assumed a boat would be in attendance to rescue her. Confidence persisted, as after all, the life belt would maintain her safety in the water for several hours.

She was one hundred feet above the water when the rate of her descent suddenly increased. According to eyewitness reports, when she struck the surface of the water a vast column of liquid rose high in the air. Both she and the parachute sank within a few minutes. Each eyewitness declared their story to be the accurate one; each account differing in essentials. Two fishermen on the shore attending their shrimp nets seemed uncertain as to what action they should take as the girl and parachute disappeared from view.

At about 9 o'clock a telegram was reported to have been received at the exhibition saying she had fallen into the sea that a boat was after her and that she had waved her hand to say she was all right.

— CHAPTER SIXTEEN —

Gaudron raced from the exhibition and set out at once in a horse drawn cab for the Moors and the Rumney River, returning forty-five minutes later, just before ten o'clock. A crowd surrounded his cab, applauding loudly, imagining Albertina had been rescued. When they realised she had not been picked up by a rescue boat there was "intense dissatisfaction" amongst the waiting group. Gaudron told a Reporter "I have been informed Mademoiselle landed in the water just outside the East Moors near some stakes and shrimping nets and has been picked up by a sailing boat from Newport which is now heading back to port."

Another story, contradicting previous reports, reached the concessionaires saying she had been picked up and taken to Cardiff Infirmary in an exhausted condition. As minutes passed with no confirmed news about the fate of the "fair young parachutist" concern turned to dread. News arrived that the balloon had been retrieved by a large crowd, three quarters of a mile from where Mademoiselle had landed in the sea. Now deposited in a field near the East Moor, in a damaged state.

As rumours of sightings began to circulate, most of which had no basis in fact, Gaudron, Mr Cundall, the executive committee and the public were in a state of unremitting suspense. Reports of a schooner having sailed to the spot where Mademoiselle Albertina landed were being sent repeatedly by members of the public to the Exhibition. Several witnesses confirmed seeing a three-masted schooner bear down in the direction of where the parachutist had fallen.

Later, when no trace of her was found, it was assumed that the boat had rescued her. It was universally agreed that Mademoiselle had ascended to a great height "becoming a dot on the mark of an exclamation". Others reported, "a fresh breeze propelled the canopy eastwards towards the vast stretch of water".

About everything else witnesses could not agree. Rumour contradicted rumour as each one gathered momentum. Sightings were reported at Newport, on the English coastal town at Clevedon and also at Weston-super-Mare, all these reports, again, challenged legitimacy.

Had she landed in the water on her back, as reported by the fishermen? Did she sink as soon as she touched the water or had she floated for some minutes? Did she wave or had there been no sign of life? Was there any acknowledgement from her to shouted greetings from the shore or had she failed to respond?

As each rumour was discounted and every reported sighting proved to be unfounded, speculation turned to rumblings of discontent. "The lady should not have been allowed to go up in such strong winds." Another observer stated "it was getting dark and the sea was a bit loppy and hard to see where she landed exactly", whilst another claimed "the time was about fifteen minutes past 8 o'clock, light fading, dusk descending, dark clouds made legitimate vision lacking in accuracy".

Previously the hero of the hour, M. Gaudron was now under siege by townspeople, visitors and the press. They all demanded an explanation as to how this accident had been allowed to happen? He needed recourse to some persuasive rhetoric. Answers were being demanded.

Why hadn't a boat been standing by in order to rescue Mademoiselle? Who was responsible for this omission? And in light of this, what were they now doing to rescue the young aeronaut? Whoever may be found responsible for the failure would need to offer a detailed explanation.

News reporters were being inundated with information from many other sources. However, their priority was to seek an interview with Monsieur Gaudron. At the time Gaudron was happy to answer their questions and to give his opinion to the press. However, this decision would be one he later came to regret.

The two fishermen, Partridge senior and his son William, who had been unsure initially as to the best course to take in the rescue, sprang into action within a few minutes of Mademoiselle landing in the water. Young Partridge was at the edge of the fishing grounds, close to the Shrimp nets and within three hundred yards of where she landed. He stated, "She came down at a great rate and dropped on her back, the water rising up twenty feet. The parachute turned over for a few minutes and then disappeared and neither the lady nor parachute was seen afterwards." He was on a mud sled and stated he saw her "fall like a tree and very, very quickly, so sudden one could hardly see her coming down."

He thought "the parachute may have failed, due to the force with which the body hit water when it could have burst the bonds of the life belt and failed her rising up". When asked the following day if he had thought of swimming out to her, he replied, "No, she was nearly a quarter of a mile out and foolish to think I could have saved her. I am not a good swimmer and I know there are strong currents about there."

Partridge Senior of 26 Wimborne Street, East Moor, "had a certainty beyond that of rumour or conjecture" as to what had occurred. He stated: "I had been standing on the Moor with friends and had seen the young woman sail over our heads towards the Channel." He said he was the first to take out a boat with a friend, Mr Rosewarne. "I got our fishing boat off the mud at the top of the Roath Dock and we pulled as fast as we could to the spot." About three-quarters of an hour elapsed between her disappearance and Partridges' boat arriving to where she had disappeared.

However, James Dunn from Rumney made a statement that contradicted the accounts given by the Partridges. He said: "whilst on the mud near the mouth of the river the woman and parachute passed over my head, carried rapidly out to sea by the breeze and landed three-quarters of a mile above the Rumney River. I called to her but had no reply."

Mr Dunn continued, "She struck the water and the parachute dragged her one hundred yards or so out into the Channel. I swam out to the spot taking about twenty minutes but found no trace of her."

Mr Walter Cook, the Exhibition Secretary and Mr McKensie, Chief Constable of Cardiff agreed: "We are impressed by Dunn's account of the parachutist landing near the mouth of Rumney River." This would have been further east than most other accounts placed her.

Although sightings were still being reported up and down the coastline of the Bristol Channel, as the lights from the docks and the Dowlais Steel Works failed to illuminate the water, and as midnight approached, the flotilla of little boats that had been searching the area for several hours returned to port.

Unsubstantiated rumours continued to circulate in the town and the next morning, Wednesday 22nd, witnesses clamoured to be heard, releasing a wealth of opinions. Fishermen, dockyard workers, train drivers, sailors and doctors each described an exact opposite to the other. Every statement vied for supremacy in its telling.

Mademoiselle Albertina's parachute had been blown off course. About that at least everyone was in agreement.

Differences in opinion arose when attributing how and where the young woman hit the water. Some insisted she had been blown at least a mile out to sea before she dropped "like a stone" into the water, whilst others stated that she "walked the water." And another, "she struck the water near East Buoy just in front of Dowlais chimneys and the Tharsis Copper Works." Most of the reports agreed that the tide was out with the exposure of "a large expanse of mudflats", and there being "quite a swell in the Channel" and "she fell into about eighteen feet of water where lots of old stakes are at this point in the river."

Information was arriving hourly at the exhibition to be assimilated by officials and the police, who were trying to sort out the wealth of reports and sightings, and to discern fact from fiction.

The coastguard at Penarth insisted he had watched "through his glass" a young woman drop into the water, after which he lost sight of her. He thought a schooner had picked her up.

David Jones, employed at Dowlais Steel Works made a statement to a reporter: "Thousands of people were gathered on the tidal field of the East Moor to watch the parachute descend." He and a companion stood on the embankment. "We had a fine view of the balloon and the woman. She worked her feet about as if trying to avoid the water. She couldn't control the wind and was carried away from the land. The parachute remained up about five minutes. The wind got underneath and turned it over on the water. It appeared to fill with water and sink. All this time the girl was moving her body and arms and seemed to be trying to extricate herself." He believed she "found her feet stuck in the mud".

The crew of the steamer *St. Davids* out of Newport saw a balloon at about 7.45pm going south eastwards. Captain

Winfield said that he and all hands watched "until we saw the parachute go down, when she seemed to drop on mud."

When asked if any boats were nearby the answer was a negative. Although he mentioned that, "four small boats put off from Cardiff and Penarth, although by then it was getting dark and a black cloud overhead." He said he couldn't see distinctly.

Members of Penarth Yacht Club witnessed the descent. "We immediately set sail in Mr Mason's yacht *Thor* and quickly reached the spot where the lady fell." They joined several punts when they all "cruised around for some time but found no trace of the lady or parachute."

John Moore of Messrs Harrison, Moore & Moore reported, "She fell in a rough patch of water and could not be seen again."

A driver of a Bute Dock Pilot engine stationed at the Roath Dock, William John, spoke soon afterwards, saying he and ten of his companions saw the balloon rise over Cardiff and the parachute descend. Wind was blowing in a north-west direction. About fifteen minutes past eight everyone became very excited as the parachute was blown over the mud "in a south-east direction and out to sea about a mile and half from shore. She struck the water and sank gradually". They called to an old fisherman, "named Partridge, his boat was a long way off on the mud. After much help from those close by the boat was pushed into the water. The fisherman rowed around the spot until dark but found no trace".

At least fifty different theories were formed. Some were

confident they had seen the parachute pass out of sight towards Newport, whilst others were equally sure that the girl fell on the mud about a mile and a quarter out and fishermen had set out to rescue her with mud sleds. Another story, which gained credence, was how she had been taken to Clevedon, whilst another rumour stated that she had been picked up by a boat near the Flat Holm.

M. Gaudron's thoughts were sought. "As the young lady's tutor, I am consumed with great anxiety." He declared, "I have fallen into the sea several times and the parachute will float for half an hour, until it gets soaked."

He was confident that the life belt she wore should have kept her afloat for a considerable period too. "Especially if the water is comparatively smooth," he vowed.

When questioned further he confirmed he had only known Mademoiselle Albertina for about four months. He continued, "I advertised for a young lady for balloon work and she was the successful applicant. She had some experience and first went up in a captive balloon with me in Dublin." He confirmed that, "since then she had descended with a parachute in Cornwall and last nights' descent was her sixth." A curious statement to make at this time, and later rescinded.

By the morning of Thursday 23rd Mr Tucker, the owner of the tug *Cormorant,* gave a statement to the press, having kindly lent this vessel the previous day. "On the afternoon of Wednesday 22nd a search party was organised. At 7 o'clock we have travelled to the locality where it was supposed Mademoiselle Albertina had dropped. Police officers were on board and had four grappling irons.

These grappling irons were used repeatedly near the fishing grounds, the supposition was that Mademoiselle Albertina may have caught in the stakes and shrimp netting. After a prolonged search over the points where it was thought any sign of the lady or parachute might be found, it proved to be without success." Two smaller boats with pilots and fishermen on board joined the search inshore. At fifteen minutes past nine as darkness made further searching dangerous, the boats all returned to Cardiff.

As reports, rumours and sightings continued to flood in to newspaper and the Exhibition Committee's offices, and despite ongoing searches being continued in the channel, pessimism took hold.

During the evening of Wednesday 22nd, twenty-four hours after her disappearance, special editions of local newspapers were published in advance of Mr Tucker's comments confirming his sad conclusion: "It is to be feared Mademoiselle Albertina the parachutist who made her first ascent from the Cardiff Exhibition last night, has become the victim of her own hazardous enterprise. In the presence of a big crowd at the Exhibition she took her place in the balloon, at the appointed hour, 7.30. She wore a nautical hat, a blouse and knickers and seemed cheery and confident. A smart breeze blew from the north-west, which had dispersed threatening rain clouds, whilst allowing clear view for spectators, carried the balloon with extraordinary swiftness towards the east.

"It is said M. Gaudron counselled the young lady to

leave the ropes of the balloon when above the Infirmary in which event she would probably alight on the East Moor.

Spectators in the Roath District said it was evident she did not act on his suggestion as the balloon sailed swiftly over the Moors and was over the channel when she appeared to come down. The balloon rose at a much greater altitude than that attained by M. Gaudron, a circumstance accounted for by the high wind prevailing.

"As she left the balloon her parachute expanded, she commenced to descend but very slowly indeed. A westerly wind tilted the parachute, the inside colour becoming visible from below. It came down very, very slowly and it was marvelled at her strength to hold on to the trapeze bar, being carried seawards.

"She struck the surface of the water near East Buoy. Witnesses said that for a while the parachute stayed open and Mademoiselle was able to 'walk the water'. After a few minutes the lady apparently disappeared. There was a swell in the channel at the time."

This report must have stunned those people who had travelled from towns and villages beyond Cardiff in order to see the lady parachutist, and had returned home before rumours began to circulate of her demise.

The news was devastating. The town was in shock. One theory being circulated which persisted, gaining some credibility, was that she had become entangled in the fishing nets, trapped between the dozens of supporting stakes covering the fishing grounds.

Yet, early on Thursday morning 23rd it was reported by

Newsboys that a telegram had been received at the Exhibition's Post Office announcing Mademoiselle Albertina had been put ashore from a schooner at Penzance, was on her way to Cardiff and would arrive at 5 o'clock. A reply from the Harbourmaster at Penzance to the telegram; "Rumour unfounded; not here." Telegrams were being despatched and answered at a frantic rate. Sent to Pier Masters at Clevedon, Gloucester, Sharpness, Avonmouth and Portishead, enquiring if any boats had "put in with the lady on board?" All responded; all with the unfortunate response "No News" and "No Tidings". Sent in hope, received with disappointment.

M. Gaudron was reported as, "still hopeful. Notwithstanding the absence of any intelligence, he speaks of course from experience and appears to rely chiefly upon precautions taken to preserve the parachutists life in the event of such an incident as falling in the water."

He stated it was impossible for the parachute to topple sideways, as claimed in some sightings. "The parachute could only fall flat on the waters' surface and would float for at least half an hour. If it was caught edgeways it would collapse and disengage itself from the aeronaut." Gaudron said it was impossible to sink whilst wearing a Board of Trade life belt, as Mademoiselle had tied around her. He'd fallen in the sea on several occasions. "What do you do?" he was asked.

"I let go the parachute, it is no weight in the water."

When asked whether, "the hoop would remain on the surface, and if the girl was also fastened to the parachute by a rope around her waist and clasps, could it be unfastened easily?"

"Yes", came the reply.

It should be pointed out, M. Gaudron chose not to be fastened to the parachute during his descents, but would use his strength to hang on to the hoop. The risk of him being pulled under the water would not apply. People continued to pontificate. Previous rumours and sightings were dismissed. Conjecture rife, the girl was "stuck fast in mud" or "entwined round stake and shrimp nets, caught fast, cold waters sapping her resolve to survive."

More fanciful and elaborate stories began to circulate; that she was "unconscious as she hit the waves from such a height, the shock having jarred the breath from her body."

And "of her heart crashing against her ribs, her lungs struggling for air as her throat filled with the soft silt and sand." With such rumours flourishing throughout the town, editors of local publications realised the public thirst for news demanded up-to-date information on this tragic event. The print presses ran for twenty-four hours at full capacity. The opinion of longshoremen and experienced boatmen at the Pierhead was that the body was not caught amongst the stakes off the Rumney River, as was supposed. The general consensus by those who understood the waters of the Channel was that the body, by now, would have been taken by the tide towards the Mouth of the Severn and Usk River.

Early morning editions of the papers began to appear on the streets and reported, "Safe to say that no event in Cardiff for many years has excited so profound and wide spread an interest (as the death now regarded as inevitable) of the lady parachutist, Mademoiselle Albertina. Her ascent witnessed by thousands of people. The whole population excited by anticipation of the balloon flight. Every man, woman and child of those thousands have naturally consuming interest in the details of the fate of one whom they had seen with their own eyes going literally to her death, as it has turned out."

Business dealings were forgotten as the commercial world became engrossed by the story, creating more enthusiasm than the previous years' General Election.

One report that gained credence was from David Roberts who was standing on the Taff Vale Railway, east of Dowlais Steel Works. "I had a glass and carefully watched her descent. She struck the water in a sloping position, her feet being lower than her head about a mile or more out from the shore." Mr Roberts insisted, "The parachute struck the sea edgeways, the wind caught it on the inside dragging her after it in the direction of the buoy."

According to Roberts, she seemed passive and made no struggle and the parachute disappeared about one or so minutes after entering the water. It twisted round and hid her from his view. Then, both disappeared.

Two sailors on board a coastal steamer watched her through powerful glasses and saw her "descend in safety until she touched the water." They witnessed "a sharp spat as her body reached the water when the parachute skidded along. It remained afloat about three minutes before it subsided into the water." They then lost sight of the parachute and the girl.

Dr W.P. Brooks believed she was insensible when she struck the water "for there was no movement of the body at all, not the faintest". This theory was endorsed by Mr Whitmell of Park Place, who stated in his letter to the Editor of the *Western Mail*, "There is one point to which attention has not yet been drawn. I refer to the possibility of severe illness produced by the rapid ascent to a region where atmospheric pressure is reduced. The height reached in such an extremely short time. It seems to me Mademoiselle Albertina was rendered helpless or unconscious by her rapid rise. In my opinion free balloon ascents, except for scientific purposes, should be forbidden. Cut off the demand and there will be no supply." He concluded, "It is as yet difficult to realise that the young girl who left us, full of life, among the plaudits of the crowd, expired in less than an hour. O, the pity of it", signed Charles T. Whitmell.

Mr Whitmell's name would remain linked to Louisa's for all time due to this letter, and a kindly act of remembrance still in evidence.

— CHAPTER SEVENTEEN —

Two days after the disappearance of Mademoiselle Albertina an extraordinary letter was written by a thirteen year old girl to M. Gaudron, whose astonishment at receiving such a missive was recorded.

The contents of the girl's letter read, "Would you kindly oblige me by accepting my company in the balloon some evening this week. I am a girl of thirteen believe me Sir, I am in earnest. Kindly let me go with you. Will you arrange an interview with me? Father and Mother consent.

Please give me an answer." Needless to say Gaudron did not respond. Neither did he reply to any of the other nine applicants who wrote requesting to be considered as replacement pupils.

However, the disappearance affected one young lady so deeply that she travelled several miles in order to stand guard at the entrance to the Exhibition in the vain hope of "meeting Mademoiselle Albertina when she returns."

The inhabitants of the town became fascinated by the tragic demise of Mademoiselle Albertina. This fascination soon turned to obsession. People gathered together, at work, in shops and street corners, the only conversation debated upon was the controversial fate of the young lady. Sales of newspapers tripled, no sooner had the *Echo* or *Western Mail* reached the newsstands and before the boys could cry out the latest headlines, crowds had gathered frantic for news.

Print runs were increased, demand outstripping supply. Every paper sold to the last copy within minutes. Morbid curiosity was partially satisfied by the thousands of people who gathered each day on the edge of Splott-lands tidal field to watch the dragging operations and searches.

Disappointment and relief was expressed in equal measure when no body was found.

Every item of every search was poured over: her name and exploits known throughout the country. Albertina's disappearance became the most talked about event.

"Practically nothing was known of her parentage, her past history as much a blank as is any trustworthy information about her present whereabouts," commented one press report. "Even M. and Madame Gaudron are in a fog about the matter."

According to the French parachutist and his wife, Marina Gaudron, the girl had answered personally an advertisement asking for a lady to undertake balloon ascents. He continued to relate the story that "she said she had been mixed up with theatrical people and in winter went with pantomimes. In summer she did turns on the flying trapeze" (an untruth that may have resulted from the interest American trapeze artist Zalva had shown in her). The Gaudrons explained, "She believed she had a mother living but could not say where she was. Her real name was Grace Parry, known professionally as Mademoiselle Albertina. M. Gaudron believed she was 21 years of age."

A hasty announcement from Mr Cundall, General

Superintendent of the Exhibition advised "that balloon ascents had been suspended and no more would take place at the exhibition for the remainder of the week." He deemed it wise to suspend the flights, "even should M. Gaudron feel inclined to make another." The Aeronaut did not feel so inclined. Even he realised that would be inappropriate.

By the morning of Friday 24th July, a further twenty-four hours had elapsed without anything of consequence being reported. The Gaudrons awoke on this, the third day to the unpalatable realisation Mademoiselle Albertina had probably drowned. Despite an abundance of information none had yielded any conclusive evidence. They must accept the inevitable. The onus was now on them to discover the girl's parentage. Someone somewhere would have to be told of the tragedy. But who? Where would they find such information? Gaudron tried to recall where the girl had lodged when she first arrived in Cardiff before taking up accommodation with Mrs Watkins in Edward Street. Perhaps some identification could be traced at Mrs Watkins' lodging house? But hadn't he been instrumental in advising Louisa where to find accommodation when she first arrived in Cardiff?

Was this a convenient pretence and cover up by Gaudron? Later it was revealed that they had discussed her being trained as an aeronaut, with the possibility of appearing with him in Scotland.

The Gaudrons crossed the street from their own lodgings to knock on the door of Mrs Watkins at number twenty–six. She welcomed the couple into the small hallway, enquiring at once if there was any news of "the poor little thing", sighing in response to the shake of Gaudron's head. She led the way up the narrow stairway as M. Gaudron expressed their hope that they might discover "some evidence amongst her belongings to help us find her relatives or friends".

The tiny space was an apology for a room, attached to the house like an afterthought with a window of similar proportions overlooking the rows of pocket gardens, where each household's privy stood in detached isolation at the top of narrow cinder pathways. A single iron bedstead pressed against the wall of the room, a quilted coverlet was pulled half-heartedly over a wafer-thin flock filled mattress. Black lisle stockings were scrunched in a careless bundle on a padded, narrow, willow-weave chair. A three-drawer pinewood chest tucked between the bed and the hanging space revealed nothing of importance, beyond a brightly coloured pamphlet extolling *The Siege of Santiago* A small bottle of eau de cologne and a hairbrush rested on top of a white crochet cotton doily. There was nowhere else to search. As the Gaudrons took their leave, the front door of number twenty-six closed softly behind them. The two landladies had found the earliest opportunity to discuss their respective lodgers and to exchange views on the missing young lady aeronaut.

The Gaudrons, Mrs Warsow informed her friend, were models of propriety and consideration, although "he being foreign had his funny little ways".

Madame was a lady of impeccable manners. And kindly too. Hadn't Madame taken in the young lady, Grace Parry, the night the girl had arrived on the doorstep at such a late hour? Insisting she sleep on the sofa, asking so sweetly for a blanket to cover the young thing, until other lodgings could be found nearby.

Pleased to repeat how she had immediately thought to tell Madame of Mrs Watkins at number twenty-six.

The couple's generosity, continued Mrs Warsow, knew no bounds. They insisted Grace take all her meals with them. Mrs Watkins, grateful for the unexpected boost of cash, was eager to register her complete agreement. She recalled how nine days before, the Gaudrons knocked her door requesting if she could accommodate their young friend, Grace Parry. "Of course I said yes immediately to such a request," recalled the landlady, anxious to satisfy such a renowned couple.

And now, what a business, indeed. The poor young woman, missing for the past three days, and hadn't M. Gaudron exhausted all possible enquiries?

Dashing here and there, chasing up the legitimacy of each rumour and every sighting, but so far, as he had confirmed this very day, without success. The two ladies declared any news would be preferable to there being no news at all.

Reporters from several newspapers were not disappointed in their search when their enquiries soon ferreted out the addresses of the two aeronauts' lodging houses. Losing no time, reporters called on the landladies, suggesting that any comments the ladies could make "would be very much appreciated".

"She said her name was Grace Parry and I understood she came from Bristol," volunteered Mrs Watkins.

"Did she say anything about her professional experience?" prompted the reporter.

"Yes," both ladies responded in agreement, "she told us she had been up several times before, and of course, we thought she had been."

Mrs Watkins continued, "I asked did her parents not mind her following such a dangerous occupation? She replied, 'Oh I have no parents now, I was brought up by my Grandmother.' I asked her in what part of the country, but the girl did not say."

Mrs Warsow thought she came from Bristol way. And added she hadn't any more information as to who the girl really was or where she was born or had been brought up.

Mrs Watkins said she had been informed that the lady had gone up five or six times before (perhaps the Gaudrons were the source of this information). Finally, both these ladies concurred they had previously expressed doubts as to that piece of information being correct.

When there was nothing more to add, the reporters departed.

Despite the search at 26 Edward Street having proved fruitless, Madame Gaudron at last recalled the address where the unfortunate girl had lodged previously. Without further delay she made the short journey to Castle Road, arriving on the doorstep of 9 Pearson Street by midday.

Fortunately the landlady, Mrs Pugh was at home. After a moment's hesitation, as Madame Gaudron explained the reason for calling on her, the landlady beckoned her into the front parlour. After a short time she returned and held out a small brown paper package. When unwrapped it revealed a carefully folded dress of shabby appearance.

Tucked into one of the pockets were two letters. Each envelope post-marked Bristol and addressed to Grace Parry, Hancock's Circus, Devonport. Madame Gaudron opened the letters without further delay. Each one headed "Crinks Tea Gardens, Conham, Bristol", written, Madame
Gaudron assumed, by the girl's mother. Despite the letters having been sent four months previously, this was the very information

the Gaudron's were seeking.

Without any further delay the couple made preparation to travel by train to Bristol. A journey during which every aspect of the tragedy and what the outcome might be, was no doubt discussed in depth.

As Madame and M. Gaudron were en route to Bristol, reporters called at 19 Edward Street, with the request to speak with Monsieur and Madame, only to be advised by the landlady "they were out early in the day and said they were not certain when they would be back". Any hope of an interview with the famous man had been thwarted for the time being.

Meanwhile the Gaudrons had arrived at Temple Meads Station by mid-afternoon. A horse-drawn cab hired for their onward journey brought them to the outskirts of Bristol and the industrial reaches of the River Avon. Eventually they arrived at the ferry crossing and the tea rooms at Conham.

Considerable time had elapsed since finding the letters at Pearson Street, addressed to Grace Parry, now they had to deliver the tragic news to the writers of these letters.

How this news was given to the Crinks has not survived. The Crinks' reaction, however, has.

The news imparted to William Crinks astonished and dismayed him. Having read of the unresolved circumstances surrounding an aeronaut at the Fine Arts Exhibition in Cardiff, his response was one of shock and sadness at the revelation. "I never imagined our Louie was the famous Mademoiselle Albertina." The Crinks confirmed that Albertina was in fact, the couples adopted daughter, Louisa Maud Evans known as Louie Crinks. Mr Crinks added that they had adopted her when she was sixteen months old but did not know her parentage – an untruth they later rescinded and denied making. She had been employed for the past four months with the Hancock family, and William Crinks had last seen her a few weeks before Easter at Taunton when he had gilded the carousels. This caused Gaudron even further consternation.

The girl he had known for four months as Grace Parry had led him to believe that her parentage was something of a mystery to her. Now it transpired she was adopted and furthermore she was born Louisa Maud Evans, later known as Louie Crinks.

M. Gaudron wondered with trepidation what else would be revealed when Mrs Crinks proffered, "Louisa was the daughter of a travelling woman named Evans. When the child was only sixteen months old, the mother, of whom now all trace is lost (another untrue statement later denied) requested that we adopt the baby girl." William Crinks took up the tale. This they had consented to do and Louie, as she then became known "was kept by me and the misses until quite recently". He continued, "Louie travelled with us up and down the country, living with us when we eventually settled down at the Conham Tea Gardens."

Further complications emerged when Mrs Crinks informed the rapidly bewildered Gaudrons that "I have a niece of mine named Grace Parry and the girl (Louie) latterly chose to take her adopted cousin's name."

No rational explanation has been discovered as to why this occurred, although one reason could be that those involved thought it prudent to keep Louie's real identity a secret. Any link to her birth mother should be erased in case the whole sorry tale of Mary Ann giving baby Louisa away just prior to the birth of her illegitimate child was exposed. The couple confirmed that a week or two before the previous Easter, Louie left them to travel and work for Hancocks' Circus. They emphasised: "not as a performer, but as a companion and general help to Mrs Hancock."

As the initial shock subsided, curiosity came to the fore. They asked whether their little girl had taken to the parachuting and what influences had been brought to bear on Louie. They wanted assurances that she had not been "pressed against her will." M. Gaudron reassured them that Grace (or Louie, or was it Louisa?) had approached him without any coercion on his part. At this point, with the advance of evening, they took their leave of the Crinks, and made haste to return to Cardiff.

What was their reaction to the news from Bristol? The story they had concocted previously about Grace Parry would have to be revised. Why, Auguste Eugene Gaudron wondered, had he spoken so freely to the press about this novice pupil. He determined he must now resist the temptation to say anything more in an unguarded moment.

— CHAPTER EIGHTEEN —

Meanwhile, in Cardiff, John Owen had been approached by a reporter from the *Western Mail* who saw an opportunity for a scoop. Was the young man who had become friendly with Mademoiselle Albertina willing to be interviewed? The reporter was in luck.

This is taken from the actual reported account. Mr Owen seemed very anxious to talk. He recalled, "That Monday evening, the night preceding the ascent, I was with Mademoiselle Albertina for some time. I asked her if she was all right as she was trembling quite markedly. I asked her if she had a mother and father who would object to her going up and she said she hadn't father or mother, but if she had, their objections would make no difference as she was determined to go."

The young fellow mentioned the matter of her nervousness again and he again advised her not to go up when she made the statement that she had some trouble or other on her mind. He continued to ask her if she had been jilted in love or anything, but she would not state what the trouble was and said, "I've got something on my mind and I'm going up. I don't care if I come down alive or not."

This statement, the reporter wrote, "puts a very strange

complexion on the already too mysterious affair." Young Owen had further conversations with the girl on the evening of the ascent, when she was fairly cheerful. He promised to go down with a cab to pick her up. She asked him to bring some milk for her to drink. She told him she always had milk after her descents. He confided, "I was determined to meet her after her flight." The interview continued, "She was humming and singing during the day and was in a good humour. She told me that blessed reporter had been bothering for an interview but she wasn't going to say anything until she came down. I suggested that she should talk about her other ascents, but she said she would say nothing until she came down. Just as she was about to start on her trip she laughed and said to me 'Don't forget the milk!' 'All right' I replied. 'Goodbye, tra la la' she said and in a few seconds she was hundreds of feet away from the earth."

He paused, looked up at the sky and spoke quietly, "I wanted her to come back safely. Where is she and why hasn't she returned?"

The press were seeking any other newsworthy comments and confirmation by the dresser that the costume and boots were "brand new" and a perfect fit for Louisa was yet further proof of a prior agreement between Louisa and Gaudron.

Proof that Gaudron already had the outfit by the time Louisa arrived in Cardiff. Despite his denials, he knew she would join him at the Fine Arts Exhibition in readiness for her appearance in Scotland.

More information came from Louisa's landlady, Mrs Watkins, who told reporters "She was in high spirits at the prospect of going up, all day on Tuesday."

Gaudron, meanwhile, must have wondered why he had lied to the press over the past few days. What could have possessed him? He was a professional, famed internationally for his daring exploits. Was he now to be brought down by a slip of a girl and by bad judgement on his part? He must have wondered whether his flourishing Aeronautic Business would suffer as a result. Publicity was one thing, notoriety, however, would put a completely different complexion on things. An element of excitement and daring brought the crowds to the venues, but endangering the life of a young girl, a novice, was pure foolishness. He regretted now the impulse to boast, as he had to several members of the press. Repeating how often she had ascended successfully in Cornwall. This was one untruth too many. The press sensed he was not telling the truth, he knew it and so did they. It would be too easy for one of these reporters to contact the venues in Cornwall and discover the real name of the lady aeronaut who had performed there.

In fact this is precisely what occurred. A reporter sent a telegram to Redruth and was informed by return that a lady parachutist had performed at fairs and fetes in Cornwall. Her name, however, was Alma Beaumont. Her final professional aerial performance took place in Torquay, after which she had travelled to London in order to be married; "a less hazardous pursuit". Where would this end? Even the girl's name was incorrect. He'd been fooled by her, and was she really only fourteen years of age? This amongst all the problems had to be the least encouraging scenario: the demise of a fourteen-year-old novice on her first ascent, under his tutelage. He could not imagine anything worse.

— CHAPTER NINETEEN —

Mary Waggett did exactly as Haycutter Little bid her: "Hurry home, as quickly as you can, and tell your parents what we have found; they will know what to do."

She needed no further encouragement and hurried back across fields and ditches as fast as the gathering gloom allowed.

Two hours had elapsed since Mary first strolled along the banks of the sea and sunlight was slipping away. She picked her way carefully over the same ground towards the distant lights of her home, happy to be able to pass on the burden of such a responsibility.

Once her mother was informed of the discovery, her concern prompted immediate action. Mary was again despatched, her mothers' voice urging her to make haste and to raise the alarm amongst the farmers gathered at the nearby Waterloo Inn.

As Mary related her tale, farmer Henry Williams hurried out heading towards the Police Station at Goldcliffe. P.C. Boucher had just returned from his evening beat and was soon acquainted with the events that had occurred at Nash. Without any delay they set out in pony and trap along the narrow country lanes to travel the three miles back to Nash Village. The time had advanced by then to approximately 10 o'clock.

Their hasty progress was hampered further when the trap in which they were travelling suffered the breakage of a shaft. As P.C. Boucher and farmer Williams made their way on foot towards Wind Bound Cottage and the Waggetts' home, they were met by several helpers from the village Inn.

The unhappy discovery by young Mary had kept them from their beds, making the policeman's request for Mary to show him the way easier. Despite the late hour, Mrs Waggett approved her daughter lead P.C. Boucher and his group of volunteers to Iron Railings Bay where the body lay still. She asked for her sister Alice to accompany her and nodded approval was quickly received from parent and policeman. With Mary and Alice acting as surefooted guides, the men followed in a more deliberate fashion, assessing each darkening field, negotiating, with care, the water-filled reens and marshland. The night relieved by pin spots of lantern-light, beams thrusting out towards the water.

The body lay, prone, arms flung sideways, feet to the sea, her head resting on a sea-washed boulder. The warm light of each lantern danced over mud and sea plants, as P.C. Boucher made a brief examination of the clothing and life belt. He called softly to the men waiting above, his urgent request to find an item suitable as a make-shift stretcher. A redundant hurdle was soon located nearby and her body was lifted up gently by strong, willing arms, before being lowered upon the wooden support. Each man took his corner of the stretcher, and with the two young girls leading, the slow, solemn procession, made progress towards Nash and the ancient parish church of St Mary the Virgin.

It was after midnight before Mademoiselle Albertina's body was laid out on a simple bier within the safety of the belfry. The medieval church a sanctuary as an improvised mortuary.

Four days before, the people of Cardiff had clamoured to catch sight of the exotic young woman, thousands had turned out to witness her daring exploits. For the past four hours she had lain, unattended, unrecognised. A bounty of the channel's changing tides, fetched up amidst timber and litter strewn boulders. There was no glamour or celebrity here.

One report suggested that after his brief examination on the mudflats, P.C. Boucher had immediately recognised the identity of the body; there could be no doubt that the young woman now lying in the quiet of the belfry was the missing aeronaut from Cardiff. Another report inclined to the theory that it was a local young farmer who, having read the story of the missing aeronaut, advised the police officer of her identity. Whichever the true account, P.C. Boucher was recorded as having remarked that he "was surprised that there was no sign of her parachute". Although he assumed "the hooks by which it would have been attached were those on her blouse still", it would transpire later during the inquest that some doubt was expressed about the function of these hooks.

Despite the unsociable hour, procedures had to be adhered to. Formalities were necessary, formal identification and attendance to certain aspects of the body required.

He deemed it politic and proper to approach Sarah Jones, licensee of The Waterloo Inn, to attend to the body. Assured by her sympathetic response – "to do my Christian duty by the young lady" – and leaving her daughter to mind the Inn, she followed the police officer through the narrow lych gate. Familiar names lit for a moment on sentinel tombstones, tender recognition fleeting, before the enveloping dark encouraged her quicker gait.

Candles surrounded the bier on which the body lay, casting high shadows on the belfry walls. The woman paused, hands fluttered in cruciform, her sudden breath staining the silent sorrow. The girls lips no longer rosy with youth, gaped wide unsullied teeth revealed white. Bruises, turned purple, blemished perfect skin. Abrasions to the scalp evidenced trauma.

A tenderly placed white 'kerchief was carefully tied round the head to secure the jaw, the perfect teeth lost from view as her mouth was secured shut. Garments in damp disarray were straightened; her slim hands, marble white were folded across her forming breasts.

Formal identification was required at the soonest opportunity. Despite reports having differed on the recognition of the body, opinion favoured that P.C. Boucher was aware of the story about the missing aeronaut, and therefore his certainty already proclaimed the answer.

Information on the articles of clothing removed from the body and taken to the constabulary at Newport by the policeman also varied, before these items were carried to Cardiff on Saturday morning for identification. The outcome, however, was the same; it was essential to formally identify the body as quickly as possible.

No matter how distressing, P.C. Boucher must perform his duties and adhere to procedures. Seawater had swollen the rope ties of the lifebelt held securely around the young woman's waist. So tight was the fit around the body it was necessary for the policeman to cut off the restrictive straps from the waist and over the shoulders. Removal of the Board of Trade lifebelt, without disturbing any of the clothing or the body was a difficult and unenviable task.

As further proof of identity, he took away the shoulder hooks and a cuff from one of the sleeves of the sailor blouse which had a band of gold braid attached.

With the help of Sarah Jones, he unlaced one of the patent ankle boots and removed a black stocking. As the sleeve was cut away, a raw graze to her right arm was exposed, indicating the body had probably made contact with either rocks, fishing stakes or metallic obstacles during the four days caught in the tidal flow of the channel. Sarah Jones smoothed back the strands of damp hair from Albertina's alabaster cheeks and tidied the unruly curls behind the girls' head. There was nothing more to be done.

Lights shone out from the open windows of the inn guiding the landlady back towards its warmth and familiar voices of her family. A single chime tolled out from the clock on the church tower; it was now 1 o'clock on Saturday morning, 25th July.

P.C. Boucher returned on foot to Goldcliffe, covering the three miles to the police station as quickly as possible.

Despite the hour, he had to write his Official Incident report of the unhappy events of the previous evening to present to his superiors at the Police Station later that morning.

"At 10 o'clock last evening I was called to Nash to investigate the discovery of a body at Iron Railings Bay. The body was that of a young woman of good features and slight build, about 5'4" in height and apparently about twenty years of age." (This information may have been suggested previously by Gaudron to the press in Cardiff). "The blue blouse, trimmed with gold, was somewhat discoloured by the water as was the pair of short bloomers.

Patent spring hooks and cord with the strap from the shoulders, to where the parachute would be secured, was firmly fixed to the life belt.

The footwear consisted of a pair of high ankle half patent lace up boots and fine black stockings covering the legs.

"Her hair," he recorded, "was loosely held together at the back of her head." He observed, "the garments and boots had a new appearance, even despite the damage by water.

The face and scalp were covered with livid patches and dark discolouration and bruising around the left eye. Superficial grazing had occurred to one arm. In the ears were small plain earrings". He concluded, "No cap or headgear was found and of the parachute there was no sign."

Finally he recorded the items of clothing, removed for identification, relieved to have completed the necessary paperwork. Shortly before noon on Saturday he took these items to the County Police Office at Newport, for inspection by his Superior Officers: Superintendent Parry and Inspector Capper. He believed that had they not recovered the body at once, it would have floated away on the morning tide, as the life belt made it additionally buoyant.

He was directed to go to Cardiff immediately, to communicate with the coroner for the division of Monmouthshire, Mr M. Roberts-Jones with a view of "making arrangements for the holding of an Inquest."

— CHAPTER TWENTY —

A meeting of the executive committee held on the evening of Friday 24th expressed a general regret at the sad fate of the lady parachutist. Chairman, Mr Forrest told committee members, "It was a feat of daring that was organised to gratify the public. It is deplorable," he insisted, "the only black spot having occurred during the Exhibition's run." As the parents of the young woman were not known a vote of condolence could not then be passed.

The Gaudrons' statement to the press that – "She had been up several times previously," – prompted a discussion amongst the committee as to how many times the aeronaut had performed such a feat. Several favoured it being her first, whilst others agreed with the Gaudrons' statement and stated it was her sixth. Asked by a member of the committee if they would allow any more ascents, a robust response from the Chairman informed them that, "they would certainly not do so, although it was a matter for the concessionaires." The debate continued as to what action the exhibition executive should adopt. It was agreed that until the unfortunate girl was found no other course of action could be taken. They would not have to wait much longer.

A special early morning edition of the *South Wales Echo* appeared on the newsstands on Saturday 25th July, reporting the news the whole community of Cardiff and surrounding countryside, did not want to read: "Intelligence received this morning came as a shock to the public mind.

It put an end to all surmises and destroyed the last faint shadow of hope, which despite all evidence still lingered in some minds."

When it was announced at the *Evening Express* that the body of Mademoiselle had been discovered, the offices were besieged with enquiries and the news spread with the "rapidity of lightning all over the town".

Nothing in recent years had caused so much interest, an interest kept alive by ever varying rumours, all of which appeared to be baseless and most of them dismissed as ridiculous. One of which even alluded to the young woman being "still alive and voluntarily in seclusion".

An earlier interview with a dock pilot, on hearing of the disappearance, expressed his opinion. "She'll have gone to the Newport River." Unhappily his prophecy proved to be true.

The only possible alteration to interfere with this theory was the behaviour of the parachute. Most sightings claimed it quickly became soaked with water and then sank, when it could have caught against stakes or other obstructions at the bottom of the channel. According to one old fisherman, "it would hold the body fast". As there was no sign of the parachute with her body, the conviction that she had either fainted or was incapacitated by giddiness on her descent before reaching the water seemed to have no foundation.

The assumption now was that she had been alive and conscious when she hit the water, and had been able to unclip the harness of the parachute. Gaudron had previously supported a statement made by a witness in *The Evening Express* that she detached herself from the parachute and then sank to a depth below the water where she could not be observed. He had been confident at that time she could swim well. Reporters were seeking him to ask his opinion. But of M. Gaudron there was no sign.

The *Western Mail* lost no time in publishing its Special Edition containing exclusive news; the body had been found. This awful news reached the Fine Arts Exhibition at Cathays Park, by 10.30am on Saturday.

The news from Nash spread faster than the papers could be printed and delivered to the newsstands. Newspaper boys were besieged and every paper was sold in minutes. At first the report was received with incredulity; so many tales in connection with the disappearance of Mademoiselle Albertina had been circulated and proved to be false. How could this young, pretty, petite lady, so smart in her exotic costume, be dead? She had looked so brave and happy as she'd climbed aboard the balloon's sling seat.

The crowds who had surged around the cycle track, and who had not shown any concerns about urging on the young aeronaut that fateful night, were now mourning her fate. Those determined to see Albertina perform had now become culpable.

A spokesman declared, "the excitement on Cardiff Exchange over the fate of the young parachutist has not been equalled since the General Election." Excitement seemed singularly unsuitable as a word of choice under the circumstances.

The news of Mademoiselle Albertina's body having been recovered at Nash swept like a tidal wave through town and countryside and, as is the way of folk at such times, the residents of Cardiff sought someone to blame; someone, whether an individual or a corporate group should be held accountable. Most accusing fingers were being pointed towards the Frenchman. Concessionaires too were berated and the executive committee did not escape the anger of the town's citizens completely. All the accusations and recriminations would not change the fact, however, that a fourteen-year-old girl had gone to her death, an object of extreme and dangerous entertainment to satisfy the public's hunger for sensationalism. Drowning in bizarre and, as the majority of people believed, avoidable circumstances. None of this had been queried previously, but now they asked, with commendable indignation, "Why had she been allowed to go up in such strong wind conditions?" And further, "Why had no arrangements been made for a tug to be on the lookout?"

These agitators insisted it must have been known that the parachute would go to sea and a tug could have been retained, under steam, for five pounds or less.

The manager of the Water Show and Concessions, Mr George Webster, confided, "I am at a loss to understand how she drowned. She must have been alive when she went into the sea as no parachute was on her. She must have removed it herself." And what of the life belt? "It was a Board of Trade belt which should have kept her afloat." It did not.

At the tea gardens in Conham, William and Mary Crinks were still assimilating the extraordinary news delivered by the Gaudrons, when on the Saturday morning the local police constable delivered yet more unhappy news. Their little girl had been found, not alive and well landed in some port or other, as they hoped, but dead, drowned.

William's pragmatic nature resolved to make immediate plans. He would catch the first available train from Bristol Temple Meads Station, bound for Cardiff, whilst Mary Crinks made haste to College Green where Mary Evans, Louie's mother now lived with Stephen Baker and their young son Albert.

The dreadful news of the death of her daughter Louisa Maud would be the catalyst for the revelation of this family's well-kept secret. The truth, so carefully concealed for so many years, would be revealed finally. Stephen Albert Baker and Mary Ann Evans had become lovers in 1882 when the two families were living a few doors from one another in Barton Hill. Whilst Andrew Evans was serving his country aboard HMS *Dragon*, William Crinks had accused Andrew of deserting his family. Contemporary Naval Service Records however established he was sailing the high seas and could have been contacted.

Mary Evans turned to Stephen's family for help when

she became pregnant with his child, begging his mother Mary Crinks to adopt her little daughter Louisa. As we know she agreed. Stephen and Mary Ann were free to live together whilst awaiting the birth of their baby.

Should Andrew have become aware of his wife's infidelity this would have been cause enough to abandon her. Although there is no proof that he did so. Twelve years later William Crinks inadvertently allowed this deep family secret to be made public. Yet the denials continued.

As Mary Crinks made her way to College Green, she wondered how she was going to tell Mary Ann that her daughter was dead.

Meanwhile William Crinks' arrival in the town during the afternoon did not go unnoticed by the ever-vigilant members of the press. No sooner had he reached the Fine Arts Exhibition, than local reporters approached him requesting an interview. He seemed happy to oblige. He confirmed he had come to take charge of the body and to see if he could be of assistance at the inquest which, as he understood it, was to be held at Nash on the following Monday morning.

Only too anxious to answer the reporters' barrage of questions he said, "his misses" had taken to the baby of a Mrs Evans, a strolling player. Mr Crinks was quick to point out that previously reported information stating that he had said he didn't know the girls' parentage was false and had been mis-interpreted by the press. He confirmed her real name was Louisa Maud Evans and anxious to offer proof of this he displayed her birth certificate. She would have been fifteen years of age on 6th December and they had adopted her when aged sixteen months. She had been born "in wedlock" but according to Mr Crinks, her father had deserted the family and gone to sea. He displayed the two letters written to Louisa by his wife, found at the lodgings in Pearson Street by Madame Gaudron Surprisingly, as no relevance was attached to these letters by the newsmen, the contents were not investigated any further.

On receipt of the unhappy news, he confirmed that his wife had straight away made to notify Mrs Evans of the death of her daughter. She had not travelled to Cardiff with him he explained, "As like ourselves she is not in good circumstances and there is no disgrace in saying that I myself had to borrow money to make the journey to Cardiff."

Questions continued to bombard the slightly bewildered man. When asked, "Then you did not know that the girl had taken to parachuting," his reply confirmed it was a complete surprise to all of them.

"Did you read the account of her ascent?"

"Yes, but I hadn't the slightest notion that Mademoiselle Albertina was Louisa Evans until M. Gaudron came to me." The questions took a different turn, "How did she leave Hancock's circus, did she run away?"

"Yes, she did."

"She talked to M. Gaudron about going on the stage in the winter, had she had any experience at all?"

"Yes, just small parts, like Willie Carlyle in East Lynne, that sort of thing."

He then produced two letters received by his wife from

the Hancocks. One, written and posted on 14th July (two days after Louisa left Torquay) said, "Louie ran away on Saturday night. She told the children (Harriet and Henrietta) that Aunt Sophie had given her five shillings, besides the money she had in her pocket, which we know to be a lie." Mrs Hancock wanted to know "if the girl was at home with them".

The Crinks replied that Louie had not returned to them at Bristol. On the 23rd (two days after her tragic balloon flight, unbeknown to the Hancocks), they wrote again from Kingsbridge in Devon. They had put the case of Louisa's disappearance, "in the hands of the police, in order to ascertain where the girl had gone." The only thing gleaned was that, "she had gone to Cardiff with the balloon man, M. Gaudron." It transpired that Louisa had told the two girls she had been offered five pounds a week (the equivalent of £300 in today's money) by M. Gaudron.

The writer of the letter then suggests Mrs Crinks should go to Cardiff "to look for the girl". The letter ends, "We have done our duty by the girl and everyone about the show was surprised when they heard she had gone."

What also emerges from these letters is they referred to her as "Louie". The Hancocks must have known her real identity.

"What sort of a girl was she, was your adopted daughter quiet or inclined to be sensational?" asked a reporter of William Crinks.

"We always found her a very good girl" he responded.

"I have never known her to tell a lie or to do a dishonest

thing", a view also held by Louisa's friends who could hardly believe that she had made a parachute decent, "being a quiet, timid girl." It was suggested also by these friends that she suffered with "a slight affliction of the heart".

William Crinks' endorsement of Louisa's honesty flies against the recorded information that she adopted a false name, calling herself Grace Parry, although this may have been at the Crinks' instigation. She pretended also to be the sister of M. Gaudron and prevaricated about her experience as an aeronaut, probably at the insistence of the French man.

As the interview drew to a close, it was agreed Mr Crinks had given his statement in a very straightforward manner and was generally sorry for the fate of his adopted daughter.

By Saturday afternoon news reporters were "hot on the trail" of Louisa's mother, with no allowance being made for her recent bereavement. Discovered at 19 Victoria Buildings in Bristol, she confirmed the statement given by

Mr Crinks the foster father. Details of the adoption was, "in every particular correct, as far as her knowledge went." An odd turn of phrase for her to use, so was Mary Ann loathe to elaborate on her personal life? Was she perhaps afraid the secret she and the Crinks shared for the past twelve years would be exposed?

Mary Ann, however, did not show the same reluctance to tell them, "my husband deserted us soon after the child was born," and that she did not know what became of him. Adding, "I always kept a watchful eye on my daughter, the Crinks being friends. I lost sight of my daughter when she entered the service of the Hancocks and I am very much upset that the young lady who ascended from the Cardiff Fine Arts Exhibition on Tuesday night was my daughter."

Andrew Evans may have been difficult to trace after he resigned from the Navy in 1888; however, this was not true whilst he was still serving in Her Majesty's Navy.

On Sunday morning 26th a letter was received by the exhibition executive reportedly from Mrs Mary Evans of Bristol (although it seems probable that she was illiterate). She had been informed, she said, that the body of her daughter had been found. The letter intimated that she intended to visit Newport on Monday when "she would be glad to receive all particulars".

A reply to the letter telephoned to the Bristol Police informed them of the time fixed for the inquest. This was conveyed to Mrs Evans who was determined to travel to Nash as soon as possible.

Travel arrangements were made for Mary Ann and her friend Mrs Crinks who had agreed to accompany her to the inquest. Reports varied as to when the two women actually arrived. One stated they travelled by train on Monday morning, from Bristol to Llanwern, a small village a few miles distance from Nash. They had then walked from the station to the Waterloo Inn arriving at the inquest after lunch. Another report suggested they travelled from Bristol on Sunday afternoon, although where they lodged overnight on the Sunday was not stated.

The fickle public's lust for sensationalism was absolved by one constant, John Owen, whose sadness of spirit dignified this young man, not contemplated by him a few hours before. The reality of loss shocked, numbed his thoughts and bound him in painful confusion.

What had she called out so plaintively to him? "Don't forget the milk", before a final "tra la la" as her voice was snatched away on the challenging breeze. A wave of her hand and she was gone.

An ache of despair accompanied him as he made his way to "Santiago", his only remaining constant.

— CHAPTER TWENTY-ONE —

When Auguste Gaudron was informed on Saturday morning that the body of Mademoiselle Albertina had been found near the entrance to the Usk River, it is claimed he "absolutely broke down". He told those surrounding him that he had held on to a tenuous thread of hope that the young woman had been picked up by a passing vessel and was alive. Despite being distressed and overwhelmed with grief he was sufficiently in control of his emotions to respond to questions about the mystery of the missing parachute. He reasoned that "when Mademoiselle fell into the water, undoubtedly the force of the wind dragged the parachute some distance from which she then disengaged herself." He was of the opinion "she trusted to her swimming powers, but had become exhausted and sank," although he insisted the Board of Trade life belt should have kept her afloat for hours. He then made his apologies, escaped further questioning from the newsmen and headed to the town centre, arriving at Cardiff Central station in time to take an early train to Newport, "in order that he might see the body for himself."

He made it known his journey to Newport was in order

to speak with the local Constabulary, where he affirmed "he considered it his duty to identify the body." To his displeasure a reporter from *The South Wales Echo* had already arrived at the County Police Station and suggested they travel to Nash together in a waiting cab. There seemed no option but for Gaudron to accept the offer, apart from displaying inordinate rudeness.

The stormy morning had given way to a serene afternoon, as the horse-drawn cab made its way from the busy docks of Newport to the rural farmland village of Nash.

The newsman noted M. Gaudron seemed extraordinarily calm in light of the fate of his unfortunate pupil. The conversation during the drive centred mainly on the tragic circumstances of his pupil. His observations of the Frenchman were such: He appeared to be about thirty years of age with a "well-kept frame and a springy step that suggested the athlete", his English spoken "with a strong foreign accent and idioms, but it is intelligible."

As the hired vehicle with its two occupants bounced over rough roads lined on either side by wide half-filled reens, the lush mid-summer vegetation sprouting out from uncut hedgerows, the spire of St. Mary's Church became visible in the distance. Nash was almost reached as the reporter, ever inquisitive asked, "How do you account for the girl sinking so quickly?"

Gaudron paused, "I cannot account for it at all." He thought for a moment, "The belt almost covered her body and should have kept her up for hours." He was not inclined to engage in conversation but seemed agreeable enough to consider each question before giving a brief answer. He confirmed he had met her when he made balloon ascents for Mr Hancock in Cornwall. He thought he had known her about two months. However, he was less than forthcoming when asked how she came to Cardiff. Whether she was with him or she had followed later, Gaudron did not make clear, although he inferred she followed him into Wales.

The cab came to a sudden halt at the half open front door of the Waterloo Inn. The shadows cast by the spire of the nearby church followed their progress. As soon as they had been welcomed into the cool interior of the inn by Sarah Jones, M. Gaudron confirmed, without recourse to further formalities, his intent to make an identification of his pupil's body, and to attend her present resting place as soon as convenient to Madame.

The cork life belt had been cut from around the waist of the corpse by P.C. Boucher and was presented to Gaudron, the material sea-salt stained. Anxious to minimise any blame being attached to him, Gaudron's first consideration was to point out to the reporter the design of the belt and the strength of the ribs – an overt attempt to confirm it was fit for purpose. The patent black right ankle boot was handed to Gaudron; a momentary hesitation belied his cool demeanour as he held the small boot briefly. Mrs Jones' kindness in having attended the girl's body the previous night was acknowledged with a smoothly rehearsed bow, at which point the key to the door of the church had been located by a willing villager.

The belfry of St. Mary's Church was a small crypt-like

rectangular vault at the base of the Church Tower. A single oak door set into the old stone work of the medieval bell tower allowed direct access from outside. Once inside the belfry, the regular shaped grey flagstones stretched over the floor towards a single window. A view of the Waterloo Inn 100 yards away. Coloured bell ropes hung from the top of the bell tower and to the left, an internal door of larger proportions gave access to the church. To the north side of the church a pathway led from entrance gates, through gravestones hidden in manicured grass, towards double wooden doors. These opened into the original entrance porch, traditional stone-carved benches on either side, as seen in village churches of similar age. On entering the church, the original Georgian box pews were immediately on view.

In this instance the two gentlemen approached the belfry from inside the church, having elected to enter the church through the porch. Gaudron's glance swept over the nave and chancel, noting a small gallery erected at the east end The seats, he observed, were plain, high backed, box-like pews as frequently found, he imagined, in village churches. At the end of the left-hand row of box pews, a wooden door opened into the belfry, where the six bell ropes dangled in the shadows of the dark interior. A single candle part lit the pallid corpse, semi-shadows played across the walls softening the gloom within the belfry. If the reporter had imagined Gaudron would display overt Gallic emotions at the sight of his young pupil laid out on the spartan bier he was to be disappointed. No reaction was discernible, no visible sign of distress from the Frenchman. "He betrays not the slightest emotion," he recorded, although the demise of such youthful innocence caused a brief disturbance of the heart's rhythm in the pressman.

He reported, "Gaudron paused, before moving towards the body. He slightly raised the head, tidied the straggle of curls, her fair ringlets spilling over the bleach-white pillow" and then stood silently until asked by the pressman if he has any doubt as to the girls' identity. He replied, "Not the slightest doubt." Gaudron showed no inclination to leave the belfry. The reporter clung to his professionalism as he took notes. The body was very slightly swollen – a result of the duration of its immersion in the water. The short upper lip exposed a perfect row of small white teeth. But the lower teeth were not visible. The handkerchief placed round the face by Mrs Jones only partially concealed a large abrasion on the left side of the scalp from which the hair had been rudely torn. A longitudinal blue mark was observable on the left side of the neck. A portion of the skin on the upper part of the right forearm had also been scraped off leaving the flesh underneath a blood-like colour.

The girls' bodice was open, displaying a frilled under garment. The corsets were folded and rested under the left arm. In her ears were small gold loops, the tiniest of circlets, but the fingers were unadorned with jewellery.

"In life, Albertina must have been attractive looking," noted the reporter. "Her face is of the oval type and her features regular, with an aquiline nose, her teeth are brilliantly perfect. As the body lies here it is incredible that it is of a girl not yet fifteen years of age."

No tears or prayers intruded upon the silence. The body of the poor girl was once more left alone in the dark of the village church. The outer wooden doors closed gently behind the two men. The key turned quietly in the lock. The silent interior of the church restored. The sextet of mute dangling bell ropes surrounded her.

The glare of sunlight stung their eyes into submission behind hastily closed lids. The only sentiment M. Gaudron permitted himself whilst passing through sun draped tombstones, a softly spoken utterance, more in conversation with himself, "I suppose that will be my fate some day."

A typical report of the period appeared in the local papers, "Albertina alive and Albertina dead was destined to be associated to the last with dangling cordage."

The "John" was hailed, from beside the inn where horse and groom had made good use of the brief leisure to quench their respective thirsts. Gaudron entered the cab with a light step – no unwelcome ghost apparently followed him inside. With the help of a local guide, the cab made progress at a steady trot towards the Waggett home.

Perched above the Usk River, the Powder Houses dominated the landscape. These protected buildings, also known as Magazine Houses, were used for the storage of explosives. Mary's father William Waggett was the Powder House attendant and custodian responsible for issuing supplies and maintaining safety regulations. Their cottage, "Wind Bound Cottage" as shown on contemporary maps of Nash, although referred to in news reports as either

"Wind Bow" or "Wind Bank" Cottage, enjoyed the addition of these industrial buildings to the frontage of their home.

Unfortunately all trace of these buildings and the Waggett's cottage have now been lost, demolished to make way for a Power Station, erected on the site during the late 1950s.

The final hundred yards were covered on foot, as the lane dwindled into a narrow pathway of grassy tufts and undulations, too narrow to accommodate horse drawn vehicles. Mrs Waggett welcomed them warmly, her young family gathered around her. Unfortunately, Mary was not at home. She had crossed over from river to the nearby landing stage earlier in the day with her father, and would not be returning until the turn of the tide some hours hence.

Mrs Waggett expressed her regret at the absence of her daughter, before courteously signifying her readiness to let her young son accompany the visitors to Iron Railings Bay.

Their disappointment was tempered immediately by the thoughtful offer.

The reporter, ever the enquirer asked, "How did your daughter chance to see the body?"

"Oh," the mother replied, "about 7 o'clock last night she said, 'Mother, I'll go round and see if anything has been washed up.' You see, just in the bay over there, things are often washed up, balks of timber from damaged ships and the like. She didn't expect to see a human body? "That she didn't sir, and she came running home terribly frightened."

The two men thanked her kindness and, led by young Walter, made their way on foot towards Iron Railings, a small irregular bay scooped out by the swirling actions of the Severn estuary.

The afternoon sun sparkled over the receding waters, exposing mud covered salty vegetation. They passed the newly built East Nash lighthouse, the resultant outcome of a lengthy agitation originated by a Captain Howe. Prior to this, the only lighthouse to guide the mariner entering the Usk in "dirty weather" was that on the West Side of the entrance, leaving him to the mercy of strong currents and treacherous shoals on the eastside.

Today the sea still ebbs and flows over the mudflats, as it did then, the seabirds wheel and dive, screeching as they search for fish. The salt marsh plants flourish and timber litters the shore, caught in the boulders' nooks and crannies. The land still protected from the onslaught of the channel's winter fury by the high stone wall. These landmarks are identifiable to the present day rambler in search of rural tranquillity and a reference to history.

They followed the broken pathway, past the Powder Houses, negotiating round a small irregular inlet with caution. The boy, the reporter and the Frenchman, an unlikely trio, bent on an unusual quest. The young boy walked directly to the spot where he had seen the body, confident of his position in the presence of two such important gentlemen. History was in evidence, the row of iron railings stretching outwards to the sea, believed, so the boy confided, to have been "put up by the Monmouthshire Volunteer Artillery for big gun practice." This spot referred to locally, still, as Cannon Wharf.

To the man from the press, the bay appeared to have been scooped out by the constant assault from the sea, leaving banks of denuded soil. The two men surveyed the scene, the quietude broken by the doleful tolling of a bell buoy. The sound floated over the muddy shallows of the estuary. In mid-July a pleasant bucolic idyll, in winter giant waves dash up this miniature bay; a mighty force unleashed against the staked embankment and sturdy stone wall, man's resistance against the rages of the sea.

Gaudron's gaze flickered over the reaches of the channel towards Cardiff. His hands lifted to shield his eyes from the sinking sun. Here, in this silent spot, the misguided girl had been cast up, putting an end to his hopes of her rescue and a happy ending to the drama. Were it not for the keen eyes of the young Waggett girl, the tide could have carried her body goodness knows where. She had drifted more than eight miles up to Nash, in all probability carried out into the full flood of the channel. Whilst the whole of Cardiff was agog with rumours and sightings, the girl's body had been floating unseen towards this small salt marsh, mudflat, boulder-strewn inlet. Gaudron lowered his hands from his face and turned back towards the footpath and Nash.

There would be questions to answer and an inquisition by the press no doubt. Mr Cundall and Mr Culley would request explanation about discrepancies in previous statements.

Mr Cundall and Mr Webster were questioned also. Did they know how many times the girl had performed? Their response: they "could not say" or "give any definite information." However, they did confirm that M. Gaudron had been approached to provide a lady aeronaut for alternative nights. The two gentlemen were very anxious to explain M. Gaudron's enthusiastic agreement, in that "he knew where to get one immediately."

They acknowledged that the bargain was made, and "no questions were asked" by either Mr Webster or Mr Cundall. No doubt they would rue this decision for the rest of their lives. Their involvement in the tragedy, however, was nothing compared to that of the Frenchman.

There cannot have been a greater game of deception than the one played out on the press and public by Gaudron. Each day, as more speculation emerged, a colourful montage of half-truths and fabrication assailed the press, until the day the body was discovered. The truth as interpreted by Gaudron then emerged.

The *Western Mail* reported consistently and captured the mood of speculation surrounding Mademoiselle. Rumours that the ascent of Mademoiselle Albertina was indeed the "first she ever made" began to circulate soon after her disappearance. Speculation aroused by her determination to avoid reporters, and her lack of inclination to be interviewed until she had been up on the Tuesday night.

An observation by the woman who helped Mademoiselle to dress: the costume and boots were brand new and the young lady did not seem comfortable "in her paraphernalia," an oversight Gaudron may not have considered if his ruse was to have been believed.

Wednesday 22nd. Gaudron had given an interview, confident that any announcement he made would be accepted without query: "Mademoiselle Albertina made many captive balloon ascents with me whilst in Dublin. She successfully ascended and descended in Cornwall by herself.

Tuesday evening was her sixth." His whimsical account debited and credited at will. When questioned about a safety harness, he said a rope was attached around her waist, as a precaution against accidents.

Thursday 23rd. Two days after her ascent, Gaudron reported that he met her four months ago at Hancocks Fair:

"She answered personally my advertisement asking for a lady balloonist, when she was engaged." Her name was Grace Parry, known professionally as Mademoiselle Albertina who, "went with the pantomimes in the winter; in summer did turns on the trapeze." He added, "She is a good swimmer if she landed in water." Was he so immersed in the fabrication that he began to confuse Albertina with Alma Beaumont?

Friday 24th. Probing questions from the press undermined Gaudron's confidence. Madame Gaudron now came to her husband's rescue, recounting Albertina's intrepid ascents. This did not quell the rumours.

He reluctantly admitted having discussed ballooning with her whilst in Cornwall, as Alma Beaumont decided to retire. She had not in fact answered an advertisement as he stated the previous day. "She clamoured to go up. She pestered me. I undertook to train her as a pupil. She had been travelling with the Hancocks' Fair for something like two months." He offered in mitigation how she had watched carefully fourteen of his ascents and descents.

"When Miss Beaumont resigned, Mademoiselle requested to take her place." The intention; she would be billed for the series of ascents due to take place in Scotland at the end of July.

Nothing he said could be disputed as no one came forward either to confirm or deny it. Whether she paid her own railway fare from Torquay as Gaudron insisted or whether from the five shillings given to her by persons unknown, it proved to be the worst expenditure she ever made.

Saturday 25th. Gaudron was interviewed in depth yet again. The game was up. His announcement that he had misled the public in saying that this had been her sixth ascent, when it was actually her first, caused a sensation. He finally admitted that she had not ascended in Cornwall at all. "It was her first time up, this Cardiff ascent was absolutely the girl's first attempt at parachuting." With rising consternation at the public's reaction to this, he reiterated he did not coerce her, she approached him. The confession continued, "Cardiff was a spur of the moment decision. Pressure placed by the Exhibition Committee to hire a lady parachutist." He was not going to take all the blame.

— CHAPTER TWENTY-TWO —

The funeral of Louisa Maud Evans would be the last chapter in a tragedy of unimagined proportions. The townsfolk of Cardiff and the country in general had suffered extremes of emotion on an unprecedented scale. The only winners during six days of mayhem had been the newspapers, as their readership increased by several thousands. And they wanted it to continue. Perhaps there was still more to be gathered from this "golden egg".

The editor of the *South Wales Echo*, keen to maintain the momentum, sent a reporter to London in the hope of interviewing someone who could keep the public's interest bubbling: Alma Beaumont.

Alma, employed for several years by M. Gaudron, could be the answer. She made her first launch from a balloon aged just twenty-one, and had undertaken at least thirty-three successful parachute descents and hundreds more balloon ascents. She was considered a most modest and courageous exponent of the art. The reporter recorded, "now married Mrs Henry Conway, an exceptional swimmer, a world champion lady high diver and expert tobogganist, as well as an expert parachutist is living at Caithness Road, West

Kensington Park." During the reported interview he constantly referred to her as "Miss Beaumont", or "Alma Beaumont, the name by which she is so well known." Her experience could throw some light on "the deplorable fate of Mademoiselle Albertina". Alma seemed happy to oblige.

A detailed description quite captured the pressman's imagination: "She is quite a little thing, both in stature and weight, not more than five feet tall and scaling less than seven stones. But she is sturdily built and her face denotes decision and firmness of character which is tempered by a kindly light in the eyes."

She acknowledged having read the report of the inquest and expressed her sympathy, "The poor child. How dreadful."

"Do you remember the girl when you were with the Hancocks in the West of England?"

"Oh yes, I remember seeing her about the place. She was a pretty girl, and looked about sixteen or seventeen."

Asked about the Hancocks she explained, "They have roundabouts and that sort of thing and organise galas on a rather big scale."

Where and when had she parted company with M. Gaudron? She thought for a moment, before replying, "On the 10th of this month, at Torquay."

Her husband interjected and answered the next question. Had she and Monsieur parted in a friendly manner? "Not quite, you see my wife is not a very good business woman and I had some words with M. Gaudron as to money matters." Mr Conway believed there was much risk involved in the profession and she should receive "a good pay accordingly." "I insisted upon this."

The reporter turned the interview back to Louisa Evans, "You remember seeing her about the Hancocks' establishment?"

"Yes, Mrs. Hancock used to call her cousin. They were related in some way." Mr Conway said he had told Mrs Hancock of a conversation he overheard between Zalva, a high-wire equilibrist employed at the show and Gaudron, plotting. "He should like to take the girl and apprentice her to his business."

Zalva is then purported to have said "being a good-looking girl, she would be a draw." Conway continued with the story, "Mrs Hancock was very angry. When I told her I thought it was a plan between Gaudron and Zalva, who were very thick together, to get the girl to become a parachutist,

Mrs Hancock was simply furious." He was convinced, "there's no doubt that was the real intention."

Whether these conversations took place is unsupported. Henry Conway may have wished to incriminate Gaudron in some way, although Gaudron did confess to having discussed the probability of Louisa taking Alma's place in Glasgow.

When asked where Gaudron was when they left Torquay on the 10th. Mr Conway stated, "He left for London a few hours before we did, but Zalva was there still." His destination may have been misunderstood, as the Gaudrons stated they went to Cardiff from Torquay.

Mr Conway explained Gaudron had entered into a contract to provide a lady parachutist in Aberdeen (this again may have been wrongly reported, as most references name Glasgow as the venue). His belief was that since his wife Alma Beaumont had now retired, "Gaudron was at a low to know where to get one so he picked upon this girl."

The intriguing information continued to flow from Miss Beaumont's husband, who seemed determined to place M. Gaudron as the villain of the piece. The bemused reporter asked, "But why did he not bring her away with him there and then?"

"Because he knew Mrs Hancock would make a row," was the explanation. He believed she might have consented to Louisa being taught to walk on the high wire, but in his opinion she would have strenuously objected to "the parachute business". He re-iterated that Zalva acted as a go-between, and that was "how the girl got to Cardiff". This may explain, to some degree, how Louisa had help with her travel arrangements and accommodation once in Cardiff.

The reporter now asked Miss Beaumont: "M. Gaudron said you were his pupil?" After a pause, and showing a degree of amusement, she replied "Did he? Well I certainly made my first parachute descent when in his employ. About three years ago."

"Had you any previous experience?"

"No, I had only handled the parachute to get used to it."

"Were you fastened to the parachute by M. Gaudron?"

"Yes, something after the fashion this girl was."

They discussed Miss Beaumont's first ascent in Glasgow, and whether there had been any mishap? None had occurred.

"Was it generally known in Glasgow that it was your first essay in parachuting?"

"Oh dear no, M. Gaudron told me not to say it was my first drop. He even instructed me as to the places at which I had parachuted, if I was asked by any of you inquisitive press men."

"And were you asked?"

"Yes, and they reported me to have performed on the Continent and elsewhere."

She confirmed having fallen into the sea at Folkestone. Despite being assured by everyone that there was no danger of her doing so, she elected to wear the life belt "as a precaution".

An important question with regard to life belts, revealed that the belt worn by Mademoiselle Albertina "was new, made by M. Gaudron, and was much larger than those worn by me. Mine was simply a few bars of cork in front; none under the arms or on the back."

"The parachute dragged me through the water and then collapsed as the gust of wind subsided.

The parachute soaked and sinking got under my legs and pulled me down. If it had not been for the cork belt I would have gone under; and it was impossible to detach myself from the parachute."

Such detailed information from an expert, who had experienced encounters in water was invaluable in understanding what may have happened to Louisa when she landed in the Bristol Channel. The newspaper report of the interview with Alma Beaumont would prove most illuminating, explaining how a parachute behaved in water and the importance of a reliable life belt.

"Did you not try to detach yourself from the parachute?" "Yes, but I could not do it at all." She explained how the rope swelled with the water making it impossible to pass through the swivel hooks. "I was finally rescued by a fishing smack after an hour or so in the water." Her expertise as a champion swimmer may have helped her survive.

"Whose responsibility in the profession would it be to pick up strayed parachutists?" Mr Conway was quick to answer "I saw the contracts with Gaudron. It was the responsibility of the proprietors to provide a trap to bring the lady back, a cart for the balloon and to make arrangements for boats to be sent out. Whilst the proprietors duty, it was equally that of Gaudron to see this was carried out too."

Then the reporter asked the crucial question: "What is your theory as to the alleged sudden disappearance of Mademoiselle Albertina, while wearing so large a life belt?" Before answering Miss Beaumont enquired, "Has the belt found on the girl been practically tested since she was picked up?"

She volunteered, "All cork does not float; an inferior cork when wet will be a burden instead of a help.

And then the girl could have become unconscious after leaving the balloon. Either by being whirled round by the hoop or the parachute not opening immediately. Whirling round has made me a bit dizzy, but I am more affected by the parachute, the swinging motion under the influence of the various winds."

"Have you any theory as to the girl becoming detached from the parachute?"

She said it was a complete mystery to her. If recovered it should not be "interfered with in any way. I can never believe she released herself from the hooks after she struck the water. I am an exhibition swimmer and even I could not do it, because of the swelling of the ropes."

She confirmed how difficult it was to get even a dry rope through the swivel hooks, an impossibility when the rope is wet, swollen by water and when "you are trying to keep afloat in the sea".

"Supposing she unhooked herself before leaping from the balloon?" "I cannot conceive she could have done even that. A girl like her could not have sustained her own weight so long a time, without falling from the parachute to the earth."

"Eye witnesses describe her having fallen into the sea on her back; is that likely?"

"Oh yes," she replied. "It depends on the wind which may tilt the parachute on to its side as it is nearing the earth or water."

As the interview came to a natural conclusion, it was time for the reporter to take his leave. He thanked Miss Beaumont. This information was invaluable. This timely interview had answered some of the questions that had arisen after the death of Mademoiselle Albertina.

— CHAPTER TWENTY-THREE —

The importance of the day was clearly understood in the Waggett house by the extent of early morning activity. Mary had been the focus of media attention for the past few days and that spotlight was not off her yet.

The morning sun promised a pleasant summer's day although the condition of the weather was not of paramount importance in the thoughts of the villagers. In fact, it was the least of considerations.

Accompanied by her father William, Mary Waggett made her way towards the Waterloo Inn and the inquest on the demise of Louisa Maud Evans. Notices had been posted in all local papers on Saturday 25th announcing, "The inquest on the body of the unfortunate girl will be held at the Waterloo Inn, Nash at 10.15 on Monday morning, before Mr M. Roberts-Jones, the Coroner for the district. Dr Hurley of Newport has been asked to make a post-mortem examination of the body and that gentleman, together with M. Gaudron and probably representatives of the concessionaires will be called to give evidence."

Father and daughter arrived in good time and made their way through the crowds of local people already congregating outside the open doors of the inn. An air of excitement generated throughout the farming community. An event of this importance had not happened within living memory.

What had brought so many people to this unremarkable village? They had left their farms and smithies unattended. Blinds were drawn down in shop windows, and notices "Closed for the day" adorned many village stores. To what end? Was the result of an inquest on an unknown young woman the sole reason for all this disruption to rural life? Or was their curiosity stimulated less by altruism and more by an appetite for sensationalism? The prospect of an illicit liaison between a young girl and a married Frenchman perhaps? If so, their curiosity would soon be rewarded with an answer. The inquest would disclose revelations and answer questions, although not as many envisaged. Once inside the inn, the Waggetts made their way towards the saloon, prepared in readiness for the official occasion by landlady Sarah Jones.

An oval table set close by the inner wall of the room, over which lay a discreet cloth of white crisp lawn. The table boasted a decanter of water encircled by several upturned glass tumblers. A pad of fine white paper, several penholders and pen nibs lay in readiness on a black pen tray, a pad of blotting paper set nearby. The heavy moulded glass inkwell was filled to the rim with black ink. The leather bound folder was over-stuffed with sets of official documents: inquisition indented forms, coroners warrant, witness depositions and jury lists. Chairs from the public bars had been placed in neat rows, in preparation for the thirteen members of the jury, the several witnesses, relatives of the girl, the press and members of the public.

Interest in the proceedings and the extraordinary story of the young woman, would render space at a premium in the cosy saloon.

The reporter from the *South Wales Argus* wrote in the strongest terms how deeply affected the public were by the tragic outcome of Mademoiselle Albertina. Impressed vividly on every memory, the inquest, he hoped, would be of a "searching character". It was up to the coroner's jury to decide if anyone was responsible for the girl's death. If so, who?

The report deplored the sad death and questioned how such dangerous feats could be performed for public wonder or amusement. "The demand for these entertainments is created by the public, a large share of the moral responsibility for any mishap must rest upon them." He expressed the hope that it would form the subject "of legislative enactment".

Mr Roberts-Jones arrival was welcomed by Mrs Jones. He had journeyed from Cardiff in the comfort of a private cab, as befitted his status: Barrister-at-Law and Coroner for the Southern Division of Monmouthshire.

P.C. Boucher, the local parish policeman, travelled the three miles from the police station at Goldcliffe by pony and trap; repairs to the broken shaft completed satisfactorily. He was relieved that provision of appointing the jury, a task that came within his jurisdiction, had been accomplished.

Thirteen good men and true were waiting in the wings to perform this onerous service to the community. Eleven jurors were appointed almost exclusively from the local farming community, whilst the twelfth member, the Reverend R. White, Vicar of the Parish and finally Walter Collett, an ex-County Councillor, who was elected as Foreman.

The first task of the jury was to accompany the coroner to the Church of St. Mary the Virgin. It was a requirement of the law that jurors view the body prior to the inquest and in the presence of the coroner, in this instance whilst it lay in the belfry of the church. Her body had suffered the effects of water during the four days whilst lost in the Channel. Another two days had elapsed since being brought to lie in the belfry. The corpse was now in a state of decomposition. P.C. Boucher mused. It was a sad state of affairs.

The police officer turned his attention back to the clusters of people gathered outside the Public House and tactfully subdued the crowds enthusiasm. To impinge on the solemn occasion with too much frivolity would not do.

Inspector Carter, representing the County Constabulary, stepped from his cab, and with a nod of recognition towards the Officer, walked through the open doors and out of sight.

Dr Hurley arrived direct from his practice in Newport accompanied by his colleague, Dr Jones-Green, who had assisted him with the post-mortem. They were anxious to take their seats before the coroner began his introduction.

As the specified time approached, with the clock

registering a minute after 10 o'clock, most of the interested parties were seated. Members of the press took their places along with an artist who would capture the essence of each witness in his sketchbook. The remaining seats were soon occupied by members of the public. The revelation of what happened to the young woman whose body lay unattended in the nearby parish church should not be missed. Those unable to secure a chair stood in close confined order at the rear of the room.

As the coroner was about to open the proceedings, Mr Webster and Mr Blackburn arrived, representing the water concessionaires at the exhibition. Taking their allotted places in front of Mr Roberts-Jones, apologies were offered for their untimely interruption.

The door to the saloon opened once again, a ripple of excitement sullied the serious proceedings, as M. Gaudron entered. Walking as quickly as he deemed appropriate, the gentleman settled into the chair beside Mr Webster.

As the clock approached a quarter past ten on Monday the 27th July 1896, the coroner's inquest into the death of Louisa Maud Evans, otherwise known as Mademoiselle Albertina, was opened before Mr Roberts-Jones, Barrister-at-Law, Coroner for the Southern Division of Monmouthshire.

Mr Roberts-Jones would probe and prompt each witness with questions raised from the depositions in order to lay bare inconsistencies. Questions and most importantly answers would be the very nub of the inquest. Highly revered, he would not countenance any duplicity. Every witness's evidence, especially that given by M. Gaudron, would require clarification for the benefit of the jury's understanding. Mr Roberts-Jones, experienced in the art of cross-examination, would know exactly how to extract the truth.

Mary Waggett was requested to stand and give her evidence. As her name was called, P.C. Boucher indicated the dead girl's relatives were not yet present. The coroner advised the assembled personages he would wait a few minutes, "pending their arrival". Mary sat quietly, the delay seemingly causing her no immediate attack of nerves. After a short delay and with no sign of the relatives, Mr Roberts-Jones directed Mary Waggett to be sworn in once again.

The following is a true transcript of the proceedings. Encouraged by the coroner, she spoke up clearly.

"My name is Mary Waggett. I am fifteen years old in three months and I live with my father William Waggett at Nash. On Friday evening between 7 and 8 o'clock, I was near the East Usk lighthouse, whilst strolling round the bank to see if there was any timber washed ashore."

She was asked what she saw there. "A body of a young girl floating in the water," was her reply. "I thought it was a man at first and it was nearly touching the land."

The Coroner then asked Mary to explain what she did on seeing the body. "I went to see Mr Little the hay cutter, to tell him a body was in the water." At this point the coroner asked if Mr Little was in the room, and was advised by P.C. Boucher that he had not been summoned to attend.

The girl recalled telling Mr Little she thought the body was that of a sailor, "because of the life jacket." Mary continued, "Mr Little accompanied me to the spot where we found the sea had washed the body on to the stones."

"What did the hay cutter do?"

"Nothing," she replied, "except walk around the body. He told me to run home and tell what I had found. I came to the Waterloo Inn to inform the men." She had made a third visit in the company of the policeman and "a lot of other people", but she didn't know who all of them were.

The jury were asked if they had any questions to ask the witness. A juryman responded, "No sir, I think she has given her evidence very satisfactorily."

Mary took her place near her father once again, her examination over. This young girl afflicted since birth by deafness, born in October 1881 three months before Louisa Maud Evans, was so close in age, yet separated by a gulf of familial experiences.

P.C. Boucher, the next witness, gave his evidence concisely whilst occasionally glancing at his notebook. He confirmed he had been notified on the evening of Friday last 24th July that a body had been washed up near Iron Railings Bay. "Found by the girl Waggett. The time was about 10 o'clock." Having gathered some men together they went directly to the Waggett family cottage, near the Powder Houses. "Where Mary pointed out the spot to me."

"I got down the bank and found the body, which was lying on some stones. The tide was out; it was pitch black and I could not see the water. The body lay on its back with its head towards the water and the feet towards the shore.

It was the body of a young woman. Tied over her blouse was a life belt." He then held the belt aloft. Members of the jury taking the opportunity to make notes whilst all assembled showed great interest in the raised garment.

"I don't think one could swim in it. It was fastened round the body and I had to cut the straps to get it off."

A juryman asked, "Is it a proper life belt? It is the only one I have ever seen like it."

Did this comment indicate it was not a regulation Board of Trade Belt? As M. Gaudron had insisted it to be on several occasions, would he be questioned closely on the subject? Alma Beaumont had also mentioned, during the interview with the reporter, that the belt was much larger than the one she used and Gaudron had made it himself, her after-thought being not all corks displayed the correct buoyancy.

The question from the juryman did not please the coroner who interrupted proceedings, telling the jury that the question, "was not relevant." He continued, "Reference to the life belt will be called upon later." But it was not.

Important information was then disclosed by P.C. Boucher, "Having conveyed the body to the church, I found underneath the sailor's blouse a strap and two hooks; the strap was put over the head and passed down the front of the body, between the legs, but not fastened behind." At which point he confirmed, "I believe the belt to be a Board of Trade regulation belt."

The foreman wanted more information about the hooks, observing, "They seemed to work very loosely."

The coroner again interrupted stating that the hooks had nothing to do with the life belt, "They were for fastening the parachute." He concluded that this would have made it easier for the girl to disconnect herself from the parachute when she reached the water. There is nothing in the report to indicate how the coroner came to this conclusion. As the inquest progressed, it became apparent he was determined to limit questions he considered irrelevant from the jury. He showed a distinct lack of curiosity.

The police officer informed the room that the life belt and other items of clothing had been taken to Cardiff on Saturday, each of which were identified by M. Gaudron and Mr Webster on behalf of the water concessionaires and the exhibition executive. A nod in agreement was observed from Mr Webster.

This concluded the police officer's evidence for the present.

M. Gaudron was called: the witness whose evidence everyone wanted to hear.

He stood, five feet, six inches tall, ever the athlete, dapper, self-assured. Speaking with a foreign accent, he began, "My name is Auguste Gaudron and my place of residence is 7 Victor Road, London." He confirmed his profession was that of an aeronaut, "With 18 years' experience."

He had known the deceased by sight for about two

months. "I saw her at Hancocks' Circus. She offered to look after the cart containing the balloon when it returned from each ascent. And I agreed." This information could not be verified as no one from the Hancock establishment was called to attend the inquest.

Whilst in Torquay, according to Gaudron, she had asked to do a parachute jump. He confirmed this happened a week before he came to Cardiff.

Before asking the next question the coroner advised the witness, "I may tell you that you are not bound to say anything which will in any way incriminate yourself."

Gaudron was asked how she came to Cardiff. This has always remained a mystery: how had an unsophisticated girl of fourteen years negotiated train services and found lodgings in a strange town late at night? He did not enlighten the coroner and jury.

"I told her I was coming to Cardiff to make parachute descents at the Exhibition. I told her I didn't want a lady parachutist in Cardiff, but I had been engaged to supply one in Scotland." He admitted, at last, he had discussed future engagements with Louisa whilst in Torquay, the suggestion being that she would appear in Scotland.

He told the coroner, the girl said she would like to visit the Cardiff Exhibition, although he didn't think "anything more about it" until she turned up at the exhibition on Monday the 13th.

Murmurs of disapproval accompanied his next response. He had no option but to confess that she hadn't come in answer to an advertisement for a lady parachutist as he had suggested previously.

This contradicted everything he had told reporters. When questioned, he strongly denied knowing, when the girl arrived or where she was staying when she came to Cardiff.

Did he not know she had arrived on the Sunday evening or where she sought lodgings? This contradicts letters sent by Mrs Hancocks to the Crinks advising them of Louisa's disappearance and stating she had gone with the balloon man. Statements by Alma's husband, Henry Conway, suggested that Gaudron and Zalva had been in competition to employ "this good looking girl."

As it seems likely that she would perform in Scotland, such important considerations about travel and lodgings would surely have been made with her before he left Torquay.

Questions were now raised by the coroner and jurymen seeking clarification of financial matters. Much was debated about whether she was to be paid.

As was his nature, Gaudron's answer was less than straight forward. "I didn't promise her any fixed salary, but she was anxious to make the descent. I would have paid her a sum for each ascent. I had engaged a lady before and paid her £5 an ascent. I had never had a fatal termination to an ascent. The girl told me she was past twenty years of age and she looked so." This flood of unsolicited responses answered several queries, and perhaps indicated his anxious state of mind.

Some confusion then arose over the years Gaudron had

been in the business. When asked, he replied, "Eighteen." And how old was he now? "Twenty-seven." Then he was nine years of age when he commenced? "No," he replied, "I was twelve."

Corrected by the coroner as only having fifteen years experience, he admitted, "It is fifteen years then."

Many theories emerged over the days before the body was found as to her aeronautic experience. The crux of which was about to be discussed. His previous suggestion to news reporters of having accompanied her in a captive balloon on several occasions whilst in Dublin was a story adapted to fit the circumstances at that time. Gaudron now advised the assembly it was she who had told him she had been up in a captive balloon in Dublin. No-one queried his change of story. Louisa had no one to fight her corner, no witnesses to speak up on her behalf from Cornwall to Cardiff, confirming or denying Gaudron's story, his interpretation, his version of how things happened. What occurred between the launch and the landing in the Channel was all conjecture. No one individual stood up to speak on behalf of Louisa Maud Evans.

Her actions on the Tuesday evening, 21st July, were criticised repeatedly by Gaudron who proclaimed, "She had jumped too late. She should have floated in the life belt. She must have unhooked the parachute. She put the swivel hooks under her blouse, so they were invisible to the watching crowds." The only voice that could have been raised against these accusing explanations was dead.

Asked had he known her name was incorrect? No, he

knew her as Grace Parry. She had chosen Mademoiselle Albertina, the name by which she would perform in Cardiff.

He admitted that he had never seen her in a balloon but she had been present at all his ascents in Cornwall, and this he considered was "sufficient experience" and should have equipped her for the flight.

When asked whether she had ever made a parachute descent, a surprisingly casual reply of, "I don't know, she didn't say," caused further disgruntled responses.

He had given her special instructions on how to act, shown her a map of Cardiff and checked how the wind was blowing, adding quickly, "In the right direction of the moors, but not the sea."

The coroner showed a level of surprise, "But it was blowing in the direction of the water?"

Pausing before admitting, the wind was blowing in the direction of the Rumney River. He continued "I told her she would not come down in the sea, but I put on the belt because you never know what will happen."

Repeating again how he told her not to go very high and to jump over the infirmary (in the middle of the town), had she done as instructed, he insisted, the wind would have carried her to the open fields.

"Did you tell her what to do if she went into the water?"

"Yes, I told her to keep to the water and unhook herself from the parachute."

If the parachutist was unfortunate enough to land in the water, Gaudron proclaimed that there was nothing to do but wait for a boat. Yet no boat was arranged for Louisa.

The jurymen who were listening intently became aware of many inconsistencies in the Frenchman's evidence. Gaudron declared he chose not to secure himself to the trapeze bar of the parachute, using instead "the strength of his hands" to hang on but Louisa, "being a lady", was secured by swivel hooks to the parachute.

The elected jurymen queried, as he was not attached, how he could speak with such authority about the problem of detaching from the canopy?

He did not respond. The coroner did not probe this further. Had she fallen into the water in an unconscious state would it be safe if the parachute was attached to her?

"Would this not be an element of danger? Would the wind not then carry the parachute through the water?" He admitted finally there was, "a strong wind blowing at the time". Although he'd played down the effect of the wind previously. Now he diverted attention away from those astute questions. Ignoring the suggestion of "an unconscious state", he insisted she would have been able to disengage herself from the 'chute.

Alma Beaumont had thought otherwise, stating in her interview with the reporter how the ropes swelled in water and had caused her difficulties in detaching the parachute on the occasion of her fall in water.

The difference in their weight was also raised. Gaudron said they had not used the same parachute as she was much lighter at seven stone seven lbs, he being two stone heavier.

How the parachute became disengaged would remain a puzzle. Theories were raised at the time and much thought has been given more recently to the mystery. No satisfactory answer has ever resolved this anomaly.

The questions continued. What time did she take off?

How high did she go? Was the height considered dangerous?

"Not dangerous," he replied, but conceded, "it was a long way from the ground."

"Did she spin rapidly?"

His reply, again, was so casual it appeared that the whole thing was of no interest to him, "I do that often. Perhaps she did." The question of who was responsible for rescuing her continued for several minutes. Gaudron refused to admit it was his duty of care to supply the boat.

"The people who engage me have to make all precaution for rescue."

"But it was you who engaged the girl not them?"

"They engaged her as well."

"They did not pay her anything?"

"No, I was to pay her."

"So the contract was with you and the girl and not with your employers and the girl?"

"It was the duty of the people who engaged me to take her out of the water."

More questions with more unsatisfactory answers. Did he know whether she could swim? How a novice such as the girl would cope with the sensations of falling from the balloon. And whether he thought her conscious when she fell into the water?

The foreman asked, "You say that you have had

eighteen years experience and you had only known the girl two months. You would not take a girl like that today or tomorrow and put her in a balloon would you?"

"If she was cautious I would."

"Is there no experience wanted?"

"No, anybody can do it. During the time I knew her she saw fourteen parachute descents."

"Do you not think a place like Cardiff was a very dangerous place to make a first descent?"

"Well a parachutist has some risk to take with every descent." To everyone's surprise he suddenly announced, "The three descents that I made at Cardiff were the most dangerous I ever made, because I could not get away from the town." Gaudron did not apparently see the significance of his statement. If dangerous for him, how much more so for a novice?

How this admission was received, by the coroner and the members of the jury, is not recorded. And no further reference is made to this statement directly, during the coroner's summing up, or in the jury's verdict. Although when it was suggested that he had taken her life into his hands Gaudron denied this, stating, "She took it herself."

He denied agreeing to pay her a salary although the letter written by Mrs Hancock to Mary Crinks refers to Louie saying Gaudron promised her £5 for each descent.

"How long before the ascent had she been announced to go up?"

"Oh, a week before." This would be the 14th July, the day after Louisa arrived in Cardiff. This was not challenged either. Had a member of the jury done so they could have established that the first mention of a lady aeronaut appeared in a press release on Monday 20th July. Despite the success of Gaudron's balloon escapades and the potential for increased revenue, the concessionaires only approached Gaudron at the end of his original contract, Saturday 18th July (four days after the date Gaudron had stated) when they suggested he be retained for a further week. The hiring of a lady parachutist was requested at the same time.

The press release on the Monday stated Alma Beaumont, the famous aeronaut, would be performing at the exhibition. The first advertisement mentioning Mademoiselle Albertino (sic) appeared one day later on Tuesday 21st. Alma's appearance wasn't mentioned again. Louisa would make her first and fateful ascent that same evening.

Other witnesses were called to give their evidence during the morning. William Crinks was sworn in and he confirmed the deceased was his adopted daughter. She would have been fifteen years old on 6th December next.

The coroner's first question, "Did she look older?"

"Well, she had grown tall with the last six years, but she had an infant look of the face at the same time." His evidence continued, in part, a repetition of the interview he had given to reporters two days previously on Saturday 25th in Cardiff. He said he last saw Louie in Taunton, a week before Easter when he had done some gilding and decorating work for the Hancocks. Asked how she came to join

Hancocks', he explained he was asked if Louie could go with them as a companion for Mrs Hancock. "I did not care for it at first, but I allowed it." Asked about Louisa's health, he replied she had never had a fainting fit as far as he knew. There had been concerns, expressed by friends of Louisa that she suffered "from an affliction of the heart."

He produced a letter from the Hancocks dated 14th July saying Louie ran away from them on Saturday night at 9.30pm, without any provocation. They did not know why she went, except that she had become "very thick with the balloon man." Indicating to William Crinks to stop immediately, the coroner remarked that that had nothing to do with the cause of death.

Before more witnesses were called, the coroner said a short recess for lunch would be taken, during which time the coroner and the thirteen men of the jury retired to a first floor reception room.

Proceedings recommenced as soon as everyone was seated once again, soon after which, Mary Evans entered the saloon supported by a police officer, the seated assembly in whispered animation. Her dramatic entrance could have done justice to a Victorian melodrama.

She began to sob bitterly and was scarcely, "able to control her emotions," according to the *Western Mail*. The coroner directed a question to the apparently distraught woman, "You seem to be much put about; she has not been living with you for fourteen years?"

Violently sobbing she answered, "Yes, but she was never out of my sight until she went with the Hancocks." Mary

Evans then exclaimed, "Look, look, look," apparently recalling the sight of her dead daughter. She grew hysterical, crying and sobbing so piteously that the coroner deemed she be relieved from any further questions for which Mr Evans must have been very thankful. However, there was an unexpected twist: Mr Crinks insisted on producing the "marriage lines" of Mary Evans – as he was inclined to call them – and placed the certificate before the coroner, his intent, it seemed, to make clear the date of Mrs Evans' marriage to Andrew. At the same moment, Mary Evans recovered her speech sufficiently to say the girl was born ten months and a fortnight after her marriage. What could have motivated these seemingly irrelevant actions? Guilty consciences perhaps afraid the past would be revealed?

As she left the room, once more with the assistance of the police, she sobbed, "Oh, dear, what shall I do, what shall I do?" Perhaps a cry for help: too little and too late.

Dr Brooks, the next witness, rose to his feet to report what he had seen. His evidence served as a useful reminder for the jury as he related the order of events as they had occurred almost a week previously.

He confirmed he lived at the East Moors, Cardiff, where he had watched the balloon ascent, "through a good glass.

She went up and was then carried away in the direction of the sea by a current of air. The parachute extended and went rapidly towards the water. At ten past eight she fell into the water."

He said, "I rushed to the edge of the bank and through my marine glass I saw her go down, about a mile and quarter from when I stood. She went down suddenly and entirely disappeared. The parachute went down on top of her."

A member of the jury asked, "Was any attempt made at a rescue?"

"No, she disappeared so suddenly, there was no time to get anything. Partridge, the fisherman and his son were fishing at the edge of the water."

Again questioned, "What did you see then?"

The parachute fell on her and the wind blew the parachute away from where I was standing. There was not the faintest movement on her part, and I did not think she detached herself from the parachute." He believed she must have gone down right through the water and the parachute gradually sank. "I saw nothing of it after four seconds. I should say that she and the parachute disappeared at the same time. She could not have disengaged herself from the parachute." Turning to the jury he continued, "She dropped on her back, there was a distinct splash in the water when she fell; she appeared quite unconscious and lifeless." At this juncture P.C. Boucher stood up to repeat what he had stated in his original evidence with regard to the hooks, the information not having attracted any attention previously. He repeated, "When we examined the body we found the hooks and these straps underneath her blouse." – he emphasised "underneath" – "They could not have been attached to the parachute at all." Gaudron disputed this immediately, saying it would have been impossible for a girl to hang onto the parachute without being hooked to the trapeze bar. She would not have had the strength. Many people had seen him at the ground attaching these hooks to the parachute. At which time the hooks were on the outside of the blouse. Finally the coroner realised the importance of the policeman's suggestion and asked the Officer, "Was there an opening in the blouse through which the hooks could pass?"

"We saw nothing of these until I took her blouse off. The blouse was firmly buttoned, or hooked over, and straps were underneath the blouse." Mr Webster (Ground Superintendent at the Cardiff Exhibition) intervened, and said, "I saw the swivels being attached to the parachute before the balloon went up. I took particular notice of the swivels."

The coroner asked Mr Webster, "When the body was recovered, the swivels were out of sight under her clothes. They were not out of sight when she went up?"

"No, certainly not. They were above the shoulders. There is not the least doubt about that."

In reply to Dr Brooks' suggestion that the ropes may have given way, Gaudron said, "These ropes are of the best Manila." Had she not been attached, as the coroner suggested, "She would have fallen in the middle of the town. Mr Webster was present when I attached her to the parachute."

Dr Brooks repeated that although she had fallen with, "a distinct splash", he believed that she was fastened to the parachute.

An extraordinary theory was then put forward by M. Gaudron: "It was quite possible she might put the hooks underneath her dress after she released herself from the parachute, so as not to let the people see she was attached to it."

It seems highly improbable that Louisa would have had the time, ability or inclination to remove the parachute, the harness and her blouse, before refitting the harness and then buttoning the blouse back over the strapping and hooks whilst treading water. All of the evidence suggests she drowned quite soon after falling in the water. Gaudron's theory that she moved the hooks herself seems to be that of a desperate man clutching at straws. How the hooks came to be underneath her blouse is never discussed in detail despite having been seen outside the blouse, prior to the flight, by several people. Nothing more was reported about the hooks or how they came to found underneath her blouse.

Nothing more was discovered during research that would help resolve this mystery or explain how the parachute became detached. Conspiracy theories abounded. None of which were proved.

One conspiracy theory favoured amongst the fishermen and dockyard workers was that a docks boatman had found her body soon after she fell in the water, had tied it to a stake far out in the channel, and awaited the possibility of a reward being offered for return of the body or information leading to such. A reward was never suggested. Four days later the body floated into the little inlet near Nash. If there was any truth in the rumour, it was never proved. The very idea was met with abhorrence amongst the good people of Cardiff when it appeared in print. Although this theory would have accounted for all the unresolved anomalies.

Mr Webster, of the Water Show and Concessions Company at the exhibition was the last witness. He confirmed he had seen the balloon ascent on Tuesday evening and at the coroner's enquiry as to whether he had engaged the girl, he was determined to make known: "No, sir; our agent was M. Gaudron." He stated that he, "took notice of the swivels."

And when asked, "Were the hooks out of sight in the dress as they were found when the body was picked up?" he was adamant in his response.

"No, sir; above the shoulders."

Dr Hurley of Commercial Road, Newport delivered the results of the post-mortem examination. His findings included "goose-skin", which he stated "would be a condition and characteristic consistent with drowning".

"There was discoloration of the forehead and a large bruise on the left side of the head." He could not say whether this injury was inflicted before or after death. "The hair was all taken off the left side. There was also abrasion of the skin of the right forearm. The heart was healthy. The lungs were inflated. In the trachea (or windpipe) was a lot of mud and sand and small particles which appeared to be sand in the bronchial tubes."

He remarked that during the post-mortem something had struck him forcibly: "There were no particles of sand or mud in the stomach. It was perfectly clean." This proved, in his opinion, "that she did not fall into the water in a conscious state. Had she swallowed any such substance she would have vomited it, and there would have been some trace of it." Therefore, he believed, "the girl was in a state of syncope (a faint), when she fell into the water.

The coroner asked, "And death was the result of drowning?"

"Yes," Dr Hurley replied.

A brief pause, "There is one thing, Mr Coroner, I should like to say. I understand there have been some suggestions made with reference to her virtue, but I will say this much, I firmly and implicitly believe that she was as pure a girl as ever lived and aught that might have been imputed to her is absolutely false." The last expression was delivered evidently, with emphasis and feeling.

This was met with unsolicited, enthusiastic applause from the gathered assembly and a heartfelt, "Hear, hear," from a member of the jury.

The coroner, precise to the last, enquired, "She was a virgo intacta?"

"Yes," Dr Hurley responded, "a virgo intacta." The equilibrium of the room needed a collective period of adjustment after the doctor's adamant statement.

Sideways glances, nodding of heads, the digging of elbows in ribs, smug smiles and satisfied murmurs of those who had known all along the girl was as pure as the driven snow, were quickly curtailed and fell silent as the coroner shifted pointedly in his chair. Mr Roberts-Jones shuffled the papers in front on him, rearranged the pens in the pen tray, sipped from his water glass. The occupants of the court waited.

The jurymen glanced towards the coroner, who stern-faced, announced he would like to proceed with his summing up. He believed enough information had been forthcoming and he advised the jurymen that there was sufficient evidence before them to arrive at a verdict. He reiterated that her correct name was Louisa Maud Evans, but that she was known as Mademoiselle Albertina whilst at Cardiff; it was supposed that she was about twenty or twenty-one years of age, but was only fourteen; supposed that she had made several previous descents, but they had heard evidence that day she had never been up in a balloon before, or descended from one. The only counter evidence they had to consider was Gaudron's statement during which he claimed that she had told him she had been up in a captive balloon at Dublin.

Mr Webster interjected, saying that she had told him this and that she had made several previous ascents and descents. The coroner immediately pointed out that there was, "not a single witness to prove that they saw her going up."

Louisa could have clarified the many contradictions. But with no one to challenge Gaudron's evidence it remained within the coroner's jurisdiction to probe further. He asked M. Gaudron if he had ever told her to say that she had been up before. The Frenchman said he had told her not to say it was the first time or else they would not let her go up.

The coroner continued, "Did you ever tell her to say

that she had been up before?"

Gaudron replied that he told her not to show herself to any reporter and not to say it was her first time.

This reply prompted the foreman to ask with surprise, "Then you knew it was her first time?"
He admitted without any embarrassment, "Yes, I knew, of course, she had not made a parachute descent." Quickly reminding the jury she had told him she'd made an ascent in a captive balloon.

As this last unexpected statement was digested by all in attendance, proceedings were rapidly reaching a point where the jury was required to discuss the evidence and arrive at a verdict. This decision was assisted by the coroner's summation, advising they would know what weight to give the evidence heard.

It would always remain a mystery how the hooks became disengaged from the parachute. Many thought, as she fell with such velocity into the water, the fall would have killed her, but the medical evidence suggested that she died from drowning.

The coroner considered it a serious matter for Gaudron to have allowed a girl of that age to go up in a balloon, especially for the first time: "If you wish to express your opinions to the conduct of Gaudron you may do so." After this, reports suggest the coroner inclined towards placing the misadventure at the feet of Louisa. He believed there was no evidence that Gaudron knew her age to be fourteen and should, therefore, not be censured. The foreman suggested that Cardiff was a rather dangerous place for a first time ascent. Referring to Gaudron's evidence, the coroner replied, "but she did not carry out the instructions of Gaudron to drop over the Infirmary."

He further indicated that had she carried out his instructions, she probably would not have landed in the water – an extraordinary statement for the coroner to have made, as no evidence had proven this. He continued, "As to being her first time, well, everybody must do something a first time." If this was reported correctly, his statement seems shocking in the extreme. Was it really the general consensus of opinion that the blame lay with Louisa?

The room was then cleared whilst the jury consulted, in private. Upon the public being readmitted the coroner announced, "The jury have returned the following verdict, that the deceased was accidentally drowned in the Bristol Channel on Tuesday last, whilst descending from a balloon."

The foreman addressed the coroner and stated that the jury, "are unanimously of the opinion that M. Gaudron displayed great carelessness and want of judgement in allowing so young and inexperienced a person to make such a perilous ascent and in such weather as prevailed on Tuesday last. And they wish me to censure you and to caution you against allowing anything of the sort to occur again."

At this Auguste Eugene Gaudron, aeronaut and professional balloonist burst into tears, turned his face to the wall and sobbed.

There would be much to discuss amongst those who had attended; and much to relate to those who had not. A verdict of accidental drowning was of little comfort to the family and friends of young Louisa Maud Evans or why this had been allowed to happen?

No one spoke up on behalf of Louisa, there was no one to contradict or agree with the evidence. The Hancocks were not called to attend, presumably having nothing relevant to contribute. And it seems they were not inclined to attend to support the Crinks or Mary Ann Evans. They did know, however, that Louisa had used the name of Grace Parry, but perhaps they were too dismayed by the deceptions and half-truths to have their names associated with the tragedy.

The only witness who could have given a true and accurate account lay, not one hundred yards away, in the belfry of St. Mary the Virgin's Church, as still and as cold as the stone carved angels in attendance. A small window in the belfry looked out towards the direction of the inn. So close to the heart of the inquest, her spirit had surely watched over the proceedings.

So many people had gathered to discuss her. Her family, her mother too. She had always hoped her mother would spend time with her one day. She must have travelled many miles from Bristol to hear the outcome of her death. She could have told them. Had that fateful flight been different she would have enjoyed the attention, all those assembled dignitaries listening to her, applauding her. Her mother, intent on hearing every word, adoptive parents too and perhaps Albert her dear half-brother. She would smile at everyone, before telling the tale of how she, Louisa Maud Evans, "Mademoiselle Albertina", had sailed in a balloon. How she had risen so fast her breath had been sucked from her lungs. How she had clung to the trapeze bar, dizzy with fear, until she took courage and jumped. Her heart almost stopped beating as she fell like a stone forever, or so it seemed, as the town rushed up to meet her. A sudden jolt had pulled her arms upwards, high above her head, releasing them from the restrictions of the cumbersome life belt. The fall into obscurity abruptly stopped, the parachute opened. Twirling and turning as her body became giddy with spinning. Nausea raced upward into her throat. The wind batted her slight frame, rippled against her thin sailor blouse and swept the parachute towards the grey-blue vastness of the sea. She would calm their anxieties. The water had embraced her, wrapping round her body. Quelling the nausea and cooling the turmoil. The parachute gently suffocated her movements, sucking her under. She had lied a little, as she had been instructed, about going up in a captive balloon at Dublin. But no harm had resulted. She regretted not telling her friend John Owen the truth. Perhaps one day, many years from now, she would be able to put that right. For a brief moment, her dreams of becoming an aeronaut had come true. Would her unsuccessful flight be remembered she wondered?

— CHAPTER TWENTY-FOUR —

Shortly after the inquest had ended, Mr Alfred Morgan, undertaker of Newport, acting on behalf of friends and relatives of the deceased girl and the authorities of Cardiff Exhibition, arrived at the Parish Church of Nash. An appropriate means of transporting the body, a shell of Elm, was carried through the stout outer door of the belfry and her body was lifted from the bier and placed inside. The trap, pulled by a single horse, removed her to Newport in preparation for the funeral at Cardiff on Wednesday afternoon.

It was no surprise, when reports emerged, "M. Gaudron it was understood would be unable to attend the funeral, having entered into engagements that week in the South of England." He had stated to anyone who would listen that he ought to have been in London that very day (Monday 27th). The report continued, "We understand that M. Gaudron has given Mr Webster the sum of five pounds for the benefit of the foster mother and father of the deceased. To cover the expenses to which they have been put." Gaudron left for London that same afternoon.

The awful demise of young Louisa continued to effect the town's population. It would not go away. The public wished to be heard. Correspondence poured forth from angry, indignant and sad observers clogging the offices of the local newspapers, children's societies and Parliament. As donations began to arrive in the post, a public subscription was set up by the *Western Mail*.

Mr Stephens took pleasure in sending £1.1s.0d towards the memorial. Mr C.T. Whitmell, who had written a few days previously condemning the tragic event and expressing his sadness, composed a tribute, suggesting an inscription for the memorial tablet. His moving suggestion submitted to the *Western Mail* would indeed become the inscription on Louisa's tomb stone.

Another letter read: "Sirs, it is intimated in your paper today that the managers at the Exhibition will forego any further parachute performances this week. A sense of propriety such as dictates a period of mourning. What is supposed to be an Industrial Exhibition appears to depend on its success for fireworks and parachute descents. Cardiff is not a suitable place for such performances. That danger might have been foreseen before Tuesday last, as the sad events of that evening demonstrated. Managers of the Exhibition ought to be indicted for manslaughter. Signed Geo.St.Clair, Castle Road, Cardiff."

The *South Wales Argus*, whose strongly worded condemnation prior to the outcome of the inquest appeared on 27th July, wasted no time in expressing its abhorrence again in the strongest terms at the outcome of the inquest, siting Gaudron, "as the culprit, his conduct beyond belief and impossible to sufficiently condemn his actions." The paper also deplored the "gaping crowd" and "people who like such entertainments," but praised the jury's censure passed upon the aeronaut as well deserved, "and he should congratulate himself on escaping so lightly." This opinion was shared and expressed in varying degrees by many others, "A young life thrown away, a child who could have hardly understood the risk she took and too young to grasp the technical theories of ballooning.

Maud Evans was a young woman alone, an adopted child a victim of other people's fortune. She ought to have met with exceptionally considerate treatment. Instead, she was suffered to throw away her life to give amusement to a gaping crowd."

The authorities in Cardiff were considered "not without blame, they should ask questions of themselves too." It was within their jurisdiction to have asserted more control over the aeronaut. The paper advocated that dangerous performances such as these needed fresh legislative enactment. With public sympathy aroused by the girls' death, lobbying against such activities could help impose restrictions. The report ended, "They pander to the worst tastes. People who like such entertainment are usually the most pusillanimous."

The sentiments of the *South Wales Argus* reported that this was a vulnerable young girl, little more than a child, manipulated and exploited for financial gain. Opportunist adults did nothing to discourage Louisa's ill-conceived ambitions. Guardians and her closest relatives failed in their duties to protect their child and secure her well being at all times.

In a week of high drama, correspondence flowed unabated. Public and official dignitaries eased their emotional tension with letters. The deluge of missives were published daily in local papers inundated with these outpourings until the press offices creaked under the weight of responses.

Donations continued to arrive in support of the Memorial Fund, administered by the *Western Mail*. A postal order for 5 shillings (equivalent to £15 today) was sent anonymously, "to contribute a little to the Maud Evans memorial fund," with the accompanying suggestion that "a balloon in the act of ascending be sculptured on the stone."

Several more letters were written condemning the exposure of children to such risk, "that they should be allowed to jeopardise their lives in senseless exhibitions."

Publishing of these condemnations served as a timely reprimand aimed at the exhibition executives and the water concessionaires; an embarrassment that would not go away. Did they rue the day they asked Gaudron to engage a lady parachutist? Their request prompted by the promise of financial gains with no consideration as to how this could be accomplished. Their worries would not be confined to published letters. With the results of the inquest published, the verdict was submitted to the Society for Prevention of Cruelty to Children. Although after lengthy considerations no case was brought against any individual, no proof established that Gaudron had known her to be under 16 years of age, the adverse publicity against Gaudron and the exhibition executive went a step further.

Mrs Gertrude Jenner's letter, dated 28th July, written to the Home Secretary, influenced the final turn of the screw. She drew the Minister's attention to the recent accident "that befell a young girl under 15 years of age." Mrs Jenner expressed an earnest wish that the Home Secretary create an Act of Parliament making illegal "such dangerous, discreditable and demoralising occupations for children of such tender years."

Her letter coincided with a question raised in the House of Commons by Mr David Thomas, Liberal M.P. for Merthyr

Tydfil, who told the same sorry tale. The Minister, Sir Matthew White Ridley, responded immediately. He would direct an enquiry at once.

On Wednesday 29th, the day of Louisa Maud Evans funeral, the *Western Mail*'s London correspondent, telegraphed Cardiff: "I understand that Sir Matthew White-Ridley has this evening despatched an order to the local authorities for the depositions taken at the inquest on the girl parachutist to be forwarded to him."

The depositions were then submitted, "for the consideration of the Law Officers of the Crown, who will advise him further on the subject." The outcome of this "consideration" was to initiate the first reading of the Dangerous Performances Bill 164, brought in by Mr Jesse Collings and Minister Sir Matthew White Ridley, on 22nd March 1897. A second reading of the Bill followed one month later in April. This proposed "an amendment to the Dangerous Performances Act of 1879 by raising the age at which children could take part in those performances from 14 to 18 years in the case of females and 16 years in the case of males."

On the 3rd August 1897 the Bill was "committed to a Committee of the whole House forthwith; the Bill reported without Amendment; read and passed". Louisa's death had brought about a dramatic change to an existing Dangerous Performances Bill. Louisa Maud Evans' legacy prompted a law that would protect vulnerable and naïve young women from seductive promises of fame and fortune. The debate in Parliament, the involvement by the Home Secretary and the reaction to the tragedy by the Society for Prevention of Cruelty to Children, sent shock waves throughout every section of the Fine Arts Exhibition. Management and committee members shrank under a welter of recriminations shaming their reputations. They would never be allowed to forget their *laissez faire* attitude and involvement in the young woman's death. Mr Webster, on behalf of the concessions, agreed they would defray expenses of the funeral.

Charles T. Whitmell's suggestion for a tribute on the memorial stone would be adopted. He wrote another letter to the editor, suggesting that the sad balloon accident could have been as a result of "severe illness produced by the rapid ascent to a region where atmospheric pressure is reduced." He had experienced "unpleasant dizziness and want of control over movements" when he had ascended to a height "above 14,000 feet" and believed it extremely probable that "Mademoiselle Albertina was rendered helpless or unconscious by her rapid ascent to such a great height." His sadness at the outcome is expressed at the close of his letter. "It is yet difficult to realise that the young girl who left us, so full of life among the plaudits of the crowd, expired in less than an hour. Signed C.T."

The inscription on the young girl's tomb stone reads:

In Memory of
LOUISA MAUD EVANS
Aged 14 ½ years

Who met with her death on July 21st 1896
On that day she ascended in a balloon
from Cardiff, and descended by a parachute
into the Bristol Channel. Her body was
found washed ashore near Nash (Mon.) on
the 24th July and was buried
here on the 29th
To commemorate the sad ending of
a brave young life
This monument is erected by Public Subscription

"Requiescat in Pace"

Brave woman, yet in years a child
Dark death closed her thy heavenward flight
God grant thee, pure and undefiled
To reach at last, the light of light. C.T.W.

— CHAPTER TWENTY-FIVE —

The Victoria car and matching pair arrived in good order and on time. Harnesses polished, coats were brushed and burnished to gleaming black perfection. A gentle trot along Commercial Road brought them to the frontage of Mr Morgan's Funeral Parlour where two mourning coaches and pair waited with relatives and friends, seated in sad contemplation.

Mr and Mrs Crinks, Mary Ann Evans, her partner Stephen and their son Albert attended in the first mourning coach – both of whom, in the name of uniformity, had adopted the name of Crinks for the occasion (as the surname Baker may have aroused curiosity as to their relationship with the deceased, perhaps inviting probing questions from the press). Whilst relatives Mr and Mrs Brooks, Mrs Wright, and friends Mrs Trimmer and Miss Honeyfield travelled in the second vehicle.

At thirty minutes past 2 o'clock, the oak coffin was borne out on a small bier, wheels of the conveyance jarring across the uneven cobbles. As the coffin was lifted into the carriage, a "handsome wreath" brought by Miss Honeyfield, a friend of the dead girl, was placed upon it. The glass surrounds of the vehicle allowed a view of the coffin and the floral tribute.

Several hundreds of local people had gathered nearby to pay their respects to the hapless young girl parachutist.

Raindrops spattered down dampening coachmen and horses as the Victoria car and mourning coaches moved slowly forward and out towards St. Mellons. A steady and seemly trot was engaged along the route. At Tredegar Park, Castleton, St. Mellons and Rumney, people came from their houses to gather and pay their respects as the cortege passed by.

As the procession of carriages reached the village of St. Mellons, their pace slowed in order to negotiate the steep hill ahead leading towards Rumney. As the top of the hill was broached, an elderly lady stepped out intent on placing a wreath on the coffin, the thoughtful tribute being handed to Mr Morgan the undertaker. Rumney Hill and the views across open fields towards the expanse of the Bristol Channel were shrouded in mist as the early drizzle turned to a downpour.

The pace was again slowed to a steady walk as the cortege descended down Rumney Hill, past the Pottery, before the road leading into Cardiff levelled, allowing a more comfortable journey for the mourners.

More and more people were gathered in silent sympathy, despite the downpour, regarded by the patient crowd as fitting on such a melancholy occasion.

At Roath Court further carriages joined the cortege: aldermen, councillors, exhibition executives, water concessionaires, Mr Cundall, Mr Webster and Mr Culley, representatives from the Santiago Choir, and Mr Whitmell (who composed the inscription for the memorial stone). An abundance of floral tributes now adorned the oak and elaborate brass decorated coffin.

They travelled past the Quins ground and the Infirmary, the crowds ever increasing. As the procession approached Castle Road, a cry went up from the hundreds of people who had waited patiently since early afternoon. The constant drizzle had not deterred them. Nothing had dampened their determination to pay their respects. There was an immediate rush by the crowds to meet the procession when a halt was made for a few moments and a magnificent wreath sent by the exhibition employees was laid beside the other floral tributes. Thousands now followed behind the procession of carriages. Mounted police waited patiently to take up position at its head. A detachment of the water concessions employees in uniform gathered around the hearse and prepared to marshal the final journey of a young woman whose impact upon them had been all too brief, but who would not be forgotten.

Was there, amongst the uniformed volunteers, a young man determined to protect her from any demonstration of over-enthusiastic attention by the crowds? Had John Owen volunteered to marshal the hearse to the cemetery?

Although not mentioned in any reports as attending, he would have been there, of that there can be no doubt. As close to his girl as he could get. A week previously, tragic circumstances denied him the honour of greeting her after her descent; now he would not leave her side until she was lowered into the ground, his last act of friendship.

The procession recommenced its journey. Reports confirmed a dense mass of people lined the thoroughfare, blinds of the houses en route to the cemetery drawn as a mark of respect, "in memory of a pure and spotless little woman who had died the death of a heroine." The hearse passed the end of Pearson Street, where Louisa had sought lodgings on her first night in Cardiff, only eighteen days ago.

Newspapers detailed the reactions of the throngs as the hearse passed bearing the wreath-covered coffin, "Strong men found it difficult to restrain their emotion, whilst old women and young women gave way to tears."

The Old World Band, who played regularly at the Fine Arts Exhibition, waited patiently at the corner of Crwys Road. At the arrival of the cortege, the mounted police indicated the band fall in behind them. Despite the rain descending in torrents, the numbers walking behind the cortege increased a hundred-fold.

Down the lane, towards the cemetery, the procession travelled accompanied by the band playing Mendelsohn's *Dead March*. The hearse, carriages, mounted police, the thousands of followers were so closely pressed together there was not a space anywhere from one side of the lane to the other.

At a quarter to 5 o'clock the cortege reached the gates of the cemetery and proceeded with some difficulty as everyone was intent on getting inside. As they approached, the bell in the tower tolled dismally. Its slow measured notes could be heard above the mournful strains of Mendelsohn's tribute to the dead. The hearse passed through the gates, the mourners at last able to enter the cemetery chapel.

Reverend R. Shelley Plant, curate of St. John's Church, centred in the town, commenced the burial service – "I am the resurrection and the life" – amid the sobs and lamentations of Mary Evans and attending relatives, the coffin was carried from the Victoria car by the marshals and borne tenderly into the chapel. A picturesque spot at the northern extremity of the cemetery had been chosen for the grave. Men, women and children three and four deep lined the pathway from the chapel to the graveside. Several hundred more had gathered around the grave, others stood on surrounding mounds and hillocks.

Mr Wolff raised his baton, summoning a final musical tribute from his bandsmen who played a solemn accompaniment as the bearers approached. Gentlemen removed their hats as the procession passed. Women dabbed moist eyes at the sight of the wreath-laden coffin supported by six young men. The Royal Epping Forest Gypsies, who had befriended Louisa when she first arrived in Cardiff, sent a fine floral tribute. And another; an arrangement in the form of a cross had been sent by M. Gaudron. A narrow pathway lead to the grave, a row of wind tossed Scots pines either side. The drip, drip of raindrops accompanied the strains of Schubert's sad composition. As the bearers approached, the crowds around the graveside fell away and the oak coffin was placed beside the deep open fissure. Reverend Plant concluded the funeral service, "ashes to ashes, dust to dust". The coffin was lowered slowly down through the freshly dug soil, posies of flowers mingled with formal tributes.

Gasps of sympathy broke the silence. Bitter tears, subdued sobbing, a last look, a mother supported by friends left her daughter to the gravediggers. Mounds of wet earth soon covered the coffin, the brass plate "Louisa Maud Evans, died July 21st 1896, aged 14 years," lost to sight. The cemetery emptied of mourners. The crowds faded away. Chapel doors were closed. Wrought iron gates padlocked. A fresh wind swept raindrops from leaf-heavy branches, each drip as the beat of a sorrowful heart. Louisa Maud Evans was alone at last and at rest.

— AFTERMATH —

The Leading Players, Buildings and Areas

STEPHEN BAKER
Mary Crinks' son from her first marriage to Albert Baker. He worked initially as a Labourer. He then changed profession and became a photographer. Married Mary Ann Evans (Fussell) in 1899. He developed his own successful ice cream and 1d lick stall business. Remarried after Mary Ann died in 1912. Born 1865. His place of birth is listed as Malpas, near Newport. Date of death unknown, but is buried with his mother Mary Crinks and Mary Ann (his first wife).

ALBERT STEPHEN BAKER
Son of Mary Ann Evans and Stephen Albert Baker. Half-brother to Louisa Maud Evans. Born 1883 in Bristol. Worked in Bristol as a labourer and a tram conductor. Married and raised four children. Died in 1956 and is buried in Bristol.

ALMA BEAUMONT
Famous Lady Aeronaut, worked for Monsieur Gaudron from 1891 to 1896, originally a professional swimmer with Capt. Roytons' Aqua Displays. Married Henry Conway in

1896. Died in the 1930s.

WILLIAM HENRY CRINKS
Born Bristol 1847/48 A fairground equipment gilder and restorer. Later added photography to his skills. Married Mary Baker, a widow, in 1880. Foster father to Louisa Maud Evans (Louie). He continued to live and work in Bristol. Died in 1905.

MARY CRINKS
Born in Bristol in 1848. Maiden name was Prigg. Married Albert Baker in Swansea in 1865. Had one son Stephen Albert Baker. Was an actress with Bakers' Portable Theatre. Married second husband William Crinks in 1880. Continued to live with William in Bristol after Louisa's death. After William Crinks' death in 1905 she lived with her son Stephen and Mary Ann. Her final years were spent in a workhouse. Died in 1907 and is buried with her son Stephen and Mary Ann.

ANDREW AIKEN EVANS
Mary Ann Evan's first husband (Jan 1881) and Louisa Maud's father (Dec 1881). Left the Royal Navy in 1888. Then worked as a coal haulier. Married a Mary Elizabeth Davies in 1891 and lived with her and their family in Mardy near Pontypridd in South Wales. They had three children, John Andrew, William Henry and another daughter he named Louisa (who would suffer from partial blindness).

Andrew Evans died in 1902 aged 42, killed by a coal truck whilst working at a coal mine in south Wales.

MARY ANN EVANS

Andrew's first wife (1881) and Louisa's mother. Born in 1863 in Keynsham, near Bristol. Second marriage to Stephen Baker (Mary Crinks son), in 1899. Their son, Albert Baker, was born six years before in 1883. She continued to live in Bristol with second husband Stephen. She died in 1912 and was buried in the same grave with Mary Crinks. On his death Stephen was buried with his mother Mary Crinks and his first wife Mary Ann.

LOUISA MAUD EVANS

Born 6th December 1881. "Adopted" by the Crinks in 1883. Given to the Hancock family (funfair entrepreneurs) in March 1896. Ran away from this family whilst in Torquay, July 11th in the same year. Arrived in Cardiff 12th July. Made her first and fatal balloon ascent and parachute descent Tuesday 21st July. Drowned in the Bristol Channel. Her body discovered at Nash on Friday 24th. Buried in Cathays Cemetery, Cardiff on Wednesday 29th July 1896. She is remembered on the official Cathays Cemetery Heritage Walks.

AUGUSTE EUGENE GAUDRON

Professional balloonist. Aeronautical business owner. Made many epic flights. He and wife Marina had a daughter who also made balloon flights. Declared bankrupt in 1909/10. Listed in Official Bankruptcy Court proceedings. Died in London during 1913. Reported as being buried in Highgate Cemetery.

WILLIAM HANCOCK

Entrepreneur, fairground owner and traveller. Famous throughout the West Country during Victorian and Edwardian period. Born 1853 in Cardiff. Married Sophie Jones. No children from the marriage. Remained at the forefront of the funfair business until 1913. Public interest waned prior to the Great War and after the war never regained same popularity. Died in 1922.

SOPHIE HANCOCK

William Hancock's sister. A character who worked alongside brothers William and Charles. Born 1854. Continued to organise the family business after its decline. Died in 1926.

CHARLES HANCOCK

William's younger brother. Born 1857. Never exhibited the same showmanship as brother William. Suffered health issues all his life. Died in 1914.

MARY WAGGETT

Born October 1881. Married a William Cripps in 1908 when aged 27. They had five children. Mary died in 1950 aged 70

She suffered with severe deafness all her life.

WILLIAM WAGGETT (Mary's father)
The Waggett family continued live at Nash. He died in 1898 two years after the Inquest.

BUTE FAMILY
The Marquesses of Bute continued to own Cardiff Castle until 1947. After the Second World War the 5th Marquess gave the castle and grounds to the city and people of Cardiff. The 3rd Marquess, John Patrick Crichton Stuart, died in 1900. Having converted to Catholicism when aged 21 years, he requested that when he died his heart should be buried on the Mount of Olives. His request was honoured by his wife.

BEESE'S TEA ROOMS
These popular tea rooms continued to be operated by the Beese family for several years after 1896. The Crinks moved to live there in 1895/6. Tea and refreshments can still be taken there to this day, accessed by ferry during summer time only. Opening times of tea rooms available via website. The area is now a very attractive country park with riverside walks. Well worth a visit.

CARDIFF
Received city status in 1905 and was declared the Capital City of Wales in 1955. The city flourished during the

Industrial Revolution boom years. It suffered during the 1960s and 1970s when the coal, iron and steel industries went into decline. Now has strong commercial, leisure and sporting reputation. A favourite capital city of tourists from all over the world.

CATHAYS PARK
Site of the Fine Arts, Industrial and Maritime Exhibition. Was sold to the Town Council in 1897 by the 3rd Marquess of Bute for approximately £167,000 on the understanding that only civic buildings would be built on the fifty acre site. No private enterprise to be allowed. Three magnificent buildings now front the area. The Law Courts and City Hall, built in 1904, and the National Museum of Wales, completed in 1927. All built in white Portland Stone.

FINE ARTS, INDUSTRIAL AND MARITIME EXHIBITION
Cathays Park, Cardiff 2nd May 1896 to 2nd October 1896. Executive committee and concessionaires were censured and received severe condemnation for failure to monitor the balloon/parachute event resulting in the tragedy. Despite record crowds attending the event, by the closure date it had made a financial loss.

ALEXANDRA GARDENS
Named after Queen Alexandra Edward VII Consort. Also now known as the Memorial Gardens housing the National

War Memorial to the 55,000 Welsh men and women killed in the two World Wars. Also memorials to the Falklands Conflict and the Spanish Civil War.

The village of Nash (near Newport) as it is today. A linear village off the beaten track.

OLD SCHOOL HOUSE
Now converted into a private residence. The village is still very rural surrounded by farmland, sheep grazing the marshland grasses.

ST. MARY THE VIRGIN CHURCH, NASH
Very much as it would have been in 1896. Old tombstones in abundance, lean at angles throughout the grassy graveyard. The interior of the church has the original box pews and balcony as described by Gaudron during his visit to the church to identify Louisa's body.

THE BELFRY
Seems not to have changed at all from contemporary descriptions given at the time. A small rectangular room beneath the bell tower gives access from the Church. Bell ropes hang down from the tower much as they must have over one hundred years ago, when used as a resting place for Louisa's body prior to the Inquest at the Waterloo Inn (a hundred yards away).

THE WATERLOO INN

The frontage has the date 1898 over its door. The interior has been updated, although the bars are small and cosy. The Inquest of Louisa was held at the Inn and it is believed to have taken place in an upstairs room, where access is no longer permitted – having become the landlord's private accommodation. Excellent Sunday lunches are now served at the inn and the landlord was extremely helpful in allowing photographs to be taken inside and outside.

EAST NASH LIGHTHOUSE

The complete original no longer in evidence, but what appears to be a slightly later version partly restored is at the same spot on the tow-path beside the banks of the Bristol Channel/Severn Estuary/Usk River.

TOW PATH TO GOLDCLIFFE

Choose a sunny day to stroll this pleasant walk. Avoid when the rain and wind are blowing up the Channel.

ROYAL SOCIETY FOR THE PROTECTION OF BIRDS

Newport Wetlands Reserve. The reens, marshland and saltmarshes are now under the protection of the RSPB. Several walks are available, commencing from the RSPB Chalet where refreshments can be taken at a small café. A shop is also on the site, and there is access to a children's outdoor play area.

WINDBOUND COTTAGE
(Mary Waggett's family home)
Demolished when the Uskmouth power station was built in the 1950s. A later power station replaced the original and access to that part of the marshlands is no longer possible. Closed in 2002.

FERRY CROSSING AT ENTRANCE TO USK RIVER
Run by William Wagget (Mary's father) until his death in 1898. The area no longer supports a ferry.

IRON RAILINGS BAY
Metal posts can be seen in the small cove where Louisa's body was washed up. These posts are believed to be the 18th century originals possibly used by the militia as target practice.

TOWN HALL ST MARY STREET
Replaced by the New Town Hall in 1904. The old town hall, replaced by "Hodge House" an office building. There is a plaque on the side of the building listing dates and architect.

NEWPORT
The town lost its coal exporting status as did Cardiff Docks. 1914 was the peak of its export. Now imports coal. Main industry it has biggest vehicle crushing operation and scrap metal export in the world.

CASTLE ROAD
Where Louisa walked to find her first lodging house. Now named City Road. A busy road with diversity of shops, restaurants and cafes.

HORSE DRAWN TRAMS
Ceased to operate in 1904 and were replaced by mechanised trams. The lines were removed during the 1950s. Now the city transport consists of buses, single and double-decker and Bendi-buses. Shopping area, known as Queen Street, was pedestrianised several years ago.

FISHERMEN/SHRIMPERS/MUD SLEDS
Stakes are still near the mouth of the Rumney River as during Louisa's time. There is still one fisherman who catches fish in the old way, by stringing nets across wooden stakes. All other fishing and shrimping has ceased.

LOUISA'S LAW (Authors' name for this Bill)
After Louisa Maud's death several letters were written to members of Parliament. When details of the event was referred to the Home Secretary. Two readings were heard in the House during March 1897 in order to bring in a Bill to raise the age of children who could appear in Dangerous Performances at Circus's or Funfairs. In August 1897 the Bill was finally passed when the age for boys was increased from 14 to 16 years and from 14 to 18 years for girls. Brought about by the death of Louisa Maud Evans, who was just 14 years of age when she died.

— ACKNOWLEDGEMENTS —

Many thanks to Jenni Chaloner for pointing me in the right direction, and Rosemary Scadden for the advice. Eleni and Kate from Cardiff Story Museum for their initial interest in this project. A special thank you to Alison Botterill for all her unflagging support and for her generosity in devoting several hours to help me amend the final draft and for all the sensible advice; to Bob Hardy who helped design the cover and to his wife Mary who supplied refreshments during the process.

Thank you to Pat Colleypriest who listened sympathetically during the ups and downs. And to John Bennett who researched Royal Navy records. For all the advice and help from Local Studies and Resource Libraries in Cardiff, Bristol and Newport especially Katrina Coopey, originally at Cardiff Central Library and more recently at the Local Studies Centre. Eric Fletcher a fellow author and "Friend of Cathays Cemetery" for being so helpful. And to my son, Julian, who read the first completed manuscript and gave a much needed critique. For his belief in the project from the very beginning and who encouraged me when my enthusiasm flagged.

My appreciation and thanks to all at Jelly Bean Books for their professional advice and support, especially a massive thank you to Hayley Cox who has guided me through unchartered waters with her expertise and unflagging patience.

— BIBLIOGRAPHY —

Friends of Cathays Cemetery Cathays Cemetery Cardiff on the 150th Anniversary (2009)
Brian Quinn *Cassini Maps Ltd* www.cassinimaps.com
E. Thomas (Photographer) Cardiff Exhibition (1896)
Souvenir of the Cardiff Fine Arts Exhibition (1896)
Julie Skinner The Francis Frith Collection
francisfrithcollection.co.uk (1890)
Kevin Scrivens & Stephen Smith Hancocks of the West – New Era (2006)
Ian S Soulsby *Cardiff, A Pictorial History* Phillimore & Co. Ltd. (1989)
William Atterton *Life in Barton Hill* Chalford Publishing Co. (1997)
T. Sackett Victorian Picture Gallery
www.victorianpicturegallery.com
Newspapers
Cardiff Times & South Wales Weekly News (24th-29th July 1896)
Evening Echo
The Graphic

South Wales Daily News
South Wales Echo
Western Mail
Western Morning News
West Briton (11/6/1896)

Libraries

Local Studies, Reference Library, College Green, Bristol
Local Studies, Dominion Way, Newport Road, Cardiff
Reference Library, Local Studies, Newport, Gwent
Glamorgan Archives, Leckwith, Cardiff
www.glamarchives.gov.uk

Hansard
www.parliament.uk

Maps

OS Map – Cardiff 1881-1882 (Reproduced from the 1881-82 Ordnance Survey Map)
OS Map – ST 1876 Cardiff (Reproduced from the 1876 Ordnance Survey Map)
OS Map – 1899-1900 Cassini Historical Maps
www.cassinimaps.com

Images

'Interior of Nash Church' courtesy of Alison Botterill
'Beese's Tea Rooms, Conham, 1890' courtesy of Phil and Lindy Leahy